An Introduction to British Economic Policy

An Introduction to British Economic Policy

Edited by

P. G. Hare
Reader in Economics
University of Stirling
and

M. W. Kirby
Lecturer in History
University of Stirling

Distributed by Harvester Press

First published in Great Britain in 1984 by
WHEATSHEAF BOOKS LTD
A MEMBER OF THE HARVESTER PRESS GROUP
Publisher: John Spiers
Director of Publications: Edward Elgar
16 Ship Street, Brighton, Sussex

British Library Cataloguing in Publication Data

An Introduction to British economic policy.
  1. Great Britain—Economic policy—1945-
I. Hare, P.G.   II. Kirby, M. W.
330.941'0858   HC256.6

ISBN 0-7108-0711-2
ISBN 0-7108-07086-6 Pbk

Src
HC
256.6
I58
1984

Typeset in 10 point Times Roman by Radial Data Ltd.,
Bordon, Hampshire
Printed in Great Britain

THE HARVESTER PRESS PUBLISHING GROUP
The Harvester Press Publishing Group comprises Harvester Press
Limited (chiefly Publishing Literature, fiction, philosophy, psychology,
and science and trade books), Harvester Press Microform Publications
Limited (publishing in microform unpublished archives, scarce
printed sources, and indexes to these collections) and Wheatsheaf
Books Limited (a wholly independent company chiefly publishing
in economics, international politics, sociology and related social
sciences), whose books are distributed by The Harvester Press
Limited and its agencies throughout the world.

Contents

List of Tables

List of Figures

Preface

Economic policy has always attracted the attention of economists and has frequently led to vigorous debates and even disputes both among economists themselves, and between economists and those more concerned with putting policy into practice such as civil servants and business managers. The policy issues regarded as most topical or most pressing at any given time obviously depend on the economic problems faced by the country concerned. In this volume, therefore, rather than covering the full range of policy issues we have chosen to be selective, concentrating on the particular aspects of economic policy of central concern to the British economy in the early 1980s. Each chapter focusses on a major issue, and concludes with some references or suggestions for further reading, and some questions for discussion.

A novel feature of the book is the inclusion of contributions from a number of different academic departments. Thus Chapter 1 is written by Professor Medhurst, a political scientist; it sets out very clearly the most important political constraints on economic policy-making in Britain, and should be borne in mind when reading some of the later chapters, particularly the ones on macroeconomic policy in Part I. Chapters 7 and 10, on industrial policy and de-industrialization respectively, were written by one of the editors, Maurice Kirby, who is an economic historian. The chapter on industrial policy was written especially for this book, to serve as an introduction to Part II, which deals with microeconomic policy. Finally, Chapter 9 on the government's various job creation schemes is the work of a sociologist, Michael Jackson. The remaining chapters were all prepared by economists.

In a book with so many authors, it would be unreasonable to expect complete agreement either in the approaches adopted or in the policy conclusions arrived at. The editors have certainly not sought to impose what could only have been an artificial uniformity. We hope, instead, that readers will find the diversity of approach both refreshing and enlightening rather than confusing and disagreeable. After all, the real world of policy-making and implementation is an extremely complex one, and we simply do not know enough about it to be able to insist that one particular approach is the only right one. The exposure to diversity offered in this book might at least discourage readers from jumping to quick and easy conclusions about economic policy where, in most cases, none exists.

The more advanced economics and related courses in schools, and introductory or intermediate courses in colleges and universities should be able to make extensive use of this book. We have assumed some familiarity with basic economic ideas and concepts on the part of our readers but have avoided technical analysis, relying on diagrams and figures to illustrate the more difficult points. However, we anticipate that most readers would also have access to one of the standard introductory texts in economic theory.

The material in this book was typed and revised with remarkable speed and efficiency, as well as with unfailing good humour and tolerance of last minute changes, by Ann Cowie. Her contribution is very much appreciated. Finally, Shirley Hewitt kindly prepared most of the diagrams and assisted in preparing the index; we are grateful to her, too.

P. G. Hare
M. W. Kirby
Stirling, September 1983

Information about the Authors

THE EDITORS

Paul G. Hare Reader in Economics. His principal research interests concern the theory and practice of economic planning. Recent publications include *Alternative Approaches to Economic Planning* (with M. Cave), (Macmillan, 1981), and *Hungary: A Decade of Economic Reform* (edited with H. K. Radice and N. Swain) (Allen & Unwin, 1981).

Maurice W. Kirby Lecturer in Economic History, with research interests including the history of industrial policy in Britain, and entrepreneurial performance in the staple industries of north-east England in the nineteenth century. He has published two books: *The British Coalmining Industry, 1870–1946: A Political and Economic History* (Macmillan, 1977), and *The Decline of British Economic Power since 1870* (Allen & Unwin, 1981).

OTHER CONTRIBUTORS

Peter Bird Lecturer in Economics, interested in welfare economics and the economics of commodity markets. Two of his latest articles are: 'Commodities as a Hedge against Inflation', *Applied Economics*, forthcoming, and 'Tests for a Threshold Effect in the Price-Cost Relationship', *Cambridge Journal of Economics*, March 1983.

Professor C. V. Brown Professor of Economics and Director of a research project for HM Treasury on the effects of taxation on work incentives. He has recently published two books, *Taxation and the Incentive to Work*, 2nd ed. (Oxford University Press, 1983), and *Public Sector Economics* (with P. M. Jackson), 2nd ed. (Martin Robertson, 1982).

Sheila Dow Lecturer in Economics, researching on monetary theory and policy, methodology, and regional and international finance. She has recently published *Money Matters: A Keynesian Approach to Monetary Economics* (with Peter Earl) (Martin Robertson, 1982) and 'Schools of Thought in Macroeconomics: the Method is the Message', *Australian Economic Papers*, June 1983.

Peter Earl Lecturer in Economics, with research interests in monetary economics and the decision-making processes of consumers, managers and economists (!) in conditions of complexity and uncertainty. His publications include *The Economic Imagination: Towards a Behavioural Analysis of Choice* (Wheatsheaf, 1983) and *The Corporate Imagination: How Big Companies Make Mistakes (Wheatsheaf, forthcoming)*.

Michael Jackson Senior Lecturer in Sociology, with research interests in trade union leadership, and employment policy, in particular the impact of special employment measures. He has published three books recently: *Trade Unions* (Longmans, 1982), *British Work Creation Programmes* (with V. J. B. Hanby), (Gower, 1982), and *Industrial Relations*, 2nd ed. (Croom Helm, 1982).

Professor Ken Medhurst Professor of Political Studies, with a general interest in the politics of Spain and Latin America (especially Colombia). His publications include *The Church and Labour in Colombia* (Manchester University Press, 1984), and 'From Princes to Pastors', *West European Politics,* 1982.

Richard Shaw Senior Lecturer in Economics and Head of Department. He also directs an ESRC supported research project on the effectiveness of competition policy. Two of his latest articles are 'Excess Capacity and Rationalisation in the Western European Synthetic Fibres Industry', *Journal of Industrial Economics*, December 1983, and 'Product Proliferation in Characteristics Space: the UK Fertilizer Industry', *Journal of Industrial Economics*, September/December 1982.

Ronald Shone Senior Lecturer in Economics. His principal research interest is in international monetary economics, but he has also published books in other fields. A couple of recent examples are: *Applications in Intermediate Microeconomics* (Martin Robertson, 1981), and *Issues in Macroeconomics* (Martin Robertson, 1983).

1 Economic Policy and Political Consensus in Post-War Britain

KEN MEDHURST

1.1 THE ECONOMIC ROLE OF THE STATE

Few students of economics would now wholly discount political or governmental factors when evaluating economic issues. There are of course debates about the impact of such factors upon economic processes, but it is now commonplace to acknowledge that politics and economics cannot be understood in isolation from each other. Economic questions are obviously high on the political agenda. Equally, political dilemmas constrain policy-makers wrestling with economic problems.

In reality, governments have never been wholly indifferent to economic matters. In this century, however, the governments of all advanced industrial societies have been constrained to involve themselves to an unprecedented extent in the running and regulation of their respective economies. They have also engaged in relatively extensive forms of international economic co-operation. By the same token, issues of an economic kind have increasingly become the subject of political controversy. Put another way, many issues once regarded as lying substantially outside the political or governmental domain have come to be regarded as proper sources of political debate or governmental concern. Thus, modern governments grappling with the great issues of recession, unemployment and inflation, all tend to concern themselves directly with matters once generally regarded as lying outside their proper sphere of interest. In the United Kingdom, the field of industrial relations constitutes a case in point. The state, therefore, partly by virtue of its own past initiatives, has now established amongst major groups or interests in our society the expectation that it is to be looked to for solutions to economic problems. Likewise, groups engaged in economic activity have shown an increasing propensity to organize themselves for the purposes of

1

defending themselves, in face of governmental intervention, or in order to get their viewpoint across to policy-makers. The CBI (Confederation of British Industry) and TUC (Trades Union Congress) are the most clearly significant products of such processes but they co-exist with a host of other business, trade union and other organizations concerned to deal with the state bureaucracy or to rally broader public support for their cause. Their existence testifies to the extent to which economic and political institutions or processes have become inter-locked and the extent to which economic matters have become politicized.

Four main and sometimes inter-related developments have given rise to this growth of the state's role. Firstly, two world wars encouraged governments, in unprecedented ways, to mobilize whole populations and entire economies for the purposes of securing military victory (Marwick, 1968). To this end, there developed novel degrees of state economic regulation and correspondingly large extensions of state bureaucracies. Victory entailed the abandonment of some experiments (food rationing for example) but some extensions of state power became permanent and compelling precedents were set. Not least, new habits or expectations of co-operation were established amongst groups once excluded from official decision-making but whose active assistance had been necessary for the successful pursuit of wartime objectives. The Second World War, for example, fostered a, for long, widely shared assumption that, irrespective of the party in power, trade-union leaders should have some access to government leaders.

Secondly, rapid technological innovations, frequently accelerated by wartime pressures, helped to create a situation of ever increasing economic interdependence that seemed to invite some degree of central control or regulation (Williams, 1971). Equally, the scale, cost and long-term nature of some activities meant that only the state was likely to possess the necessary resources. This might be true, for example, of developments in the energy field.

Thirdly, inter-war experience of the slump and massive depression gave rise, after 1945, to a widely shared assumption that governments (again, to a significant degree, irrespective of party) had a general responsibility for so managing the economy that expansion would be sustained, drifts into recession checked and unemployment, as a consequence, minimized (Beer, 1969). For these purposes it was felt sufficient to implement Keynesian economic theories which stressed management of total or aggregate demand within the economy, rather than detailed state intervention or economic planning. The state's role, it was generally understood, was to stimulate demand (or stave off over-production) through use of its control over taxation levels, credit policies and its own public expenditure programmes. Its function in other words was, for the most part, to create appropriate conditions within which the private sector could develop and make judicious investment decisions. Its function was not to plan in any detail the specific activities of given economic sectors, still less of individual enterprises. Put another way, such forms of economic management were perceived as a way of preserving (albeit in modified form) the established capitalist market system which, during the great depression, had seemed threatened. Likewise, they were seen as ways of avoiding political upheavals of the sort that occurred in Germany in the early 1930s or that could mobilize support for largely state controlled (or 'command') economies of the Soviet variety.

Fourthly long-term political developments, within the context of industrial society, led to the emergence of political movements responsive to working-class pressures, and demanded a degree of public ownership within the economy and conscious efforts, through state-sponsored welfare programmes, to combat the inequalities of wealth and opportunity resulting from inherited class structures or from the operations of the market. In Britain the Labour government of 1945 signified something of a watershed in such strivings for a permanently enhanced state economic and welfare role (see Addison, 1975). Some of that government's reforms implemented agreements reached within the wartime coalition. Nevertheless, they signified a new acceptance of the importance of the Labour movement in British politics and of the need to take serious account of its aspirations and interests. The net result (through the nationalization of the railways, coal mining and other activities) was to accentuate the state's role as an employer or producer and firmly to establish the 'mixed economy' characteristic of post-war Britain. The effect was also greatly to increase the scale of government expenditure so that it tended to account for an ever-increasing proportion of the nation's total resources. Indeed, until the late 1970s governments of both major parties, albeit with differing emphases, presided over the continuing development of a 'welfare state'. It became an apparently fixed principle that the state had responsibility for ensuring universal health care, education, acceptable housing and for preventing the worst forms or consequences of poverty.

1.2 THE 'POST-WAR CONSENSUS'

As already stressed, a significant degree of agreement or 'consensus' emerged between the major British political parties concerning this post-war 'political settlement'. In opposition after 1945, the Conservative party's leadership reconsidered established positions and when returned to office in 1951, did relatively little to reverse Labour's major reforms. Indeed, the 1950s and early 1960s witnessed a period of so called 'Butskellism' (named after Labour and Conservative chancellors of the exchequer, Gaitskell and Butler) during which the Treasury's general pattern of economic management reflected certain underlying continuities. Conservative apologists tended to see this as evidence of a characteristically fruitful pragmatism that enabled them successfully to adjust to prevailing realities. They also tended to see the general assumption of state responsibility for economic prosperity and public welfare as an expression of long-established Conservative ideas concerning the maintenance of national unity and the need for more favoured social sectors to show some care for the less favoured. By contrast, more radical Labour elements tended then, and subsequently, to argue that the balance of public and private economic power had been relatively little changed and that conflicts of interest engendered within a still largely market economy were being masked rather than resolved through post-war policies.

Initially such questionings made little headway. Internal Labour party controversy tended, for a time, principally to focus on defence rather than economic issues. Moreover, successive Conservative election victories seemed to signify substantial satisfaction with the status quo. Some commentators even began to doubt the relevance of existing Labour party commitments and its long-term chances of regaining office. Some argued against the appropriateness of further extensions of public ownership and suggested that the major issue was the use of the state to effect more drastic redistributions of wealth within the framework of existing economic relationships rather than radically questioning such relationships (Crosland, 1964). Gaitskell, as Labour leader, strived (unsuccessfully) to abandon Labour's official commitment to nationalization (see Minkin, 1978). His successor, Harold Wilson, chose largely to ignore this divisive issue but opted instead to rally his party in temporarily united support of a 'modernizing' programme that might appeal to the electorate, across class lines, and that promised, particularly through the harnessing of science and technology, to make more efficient use of existing resources and institutions. Even then, the Labour party only returned to office in 1964 with a slender parliamentary majority, and had to wait until 1966 for a substantial electoral victory.

Such developments occurred against the background of a period of apparently successful post-war economic recovery – recovery which proved electorally advantageous to the Conservative party but which also appeared to confirm the solidity of post-war economic arrangements. During the 1960s unprecedented levels of British prosperity, in which most social sectors had some share, seemed to confirm the adequacy of prevailing forms of official economic management.

On the other hand the late 1950s and early 1960s saw the beginnings of some disquiet amongst portions of the nation's political and business leadership. They were aware that domestic prosperity which, in absolute terms, was unrivalled, coexisted with a decline in Britain's relative economic standing in the world at large. In other words the British economy was clearly proving to be less productive and competitive than its major industrial counterparts so that actual or potential overseas markets were lost and the domestic market was liable to be penetrated by non-British goods. Likewise, business operated in a climate of some uncertainty associated with so called 'stop-go' policies whereby periods of boom alternated with periods of contraction (Brittan, 1974). A perennial problem seemed to be that in periods of expanding domestic activity imports flooded into the country. These supplied industry's raw material needs and satisfied internal consumer demands, but had adverse consequences for the country's balance of payments and for confidence in the standing of sterling as an international medium of exchange. Thus spurts of growth (which thanks to government intervention tended to precede elections) were subsequently paid for by government inspired restrictions upon consumer demand in the shape of measures such as credit restrictions or tax increases. In these circumstances such existing business weaknesses as reluctance to pursue planned investment strategies and to abandon obsolete practices, were perhaps exacerbated.

The problem of regeneration was particularly significant given the extent and speed of technological change which tended to accelerate the decline of long established or basic industries associated with Britain's early industrial success. Equally, some of these industries, textiles for example, were adversely affected by foreign competition. The result was a worsening of regional imbalances in Britain and growing concentrations of unemployment within particular areas (not least areas in which the Labour movement had some of its strongest roots).

The debate engendered by growing awareness of such dilemmas led first Conservative governments and then their Labour successors to experiment with some new institutional devices (see Shonfield, 1976, esp. chs 5–8). Thus machinery was established providing for regular tripartite discussions between government, business and labour with a view to mobilizing general support for agreed expansionary policies. Likewise, attempts were made to emulate apparently successful post-war French experiments in so called 'indicative planning'. These involved the state in detailed consultations with business and labour in order to establish firm guidelines for industry to follow in making their investment decisions. Within the private sector such guidelines were not regarded as mandatory but as general indications of the course to be pursued. The state, by contrast, was expected to adhere closely to planned targets in order to foster a climate of relatively certain economic expectations and business confidence. Specialists debate the extent to which French economic recovery flowed from or occurred in spite of such arrangements (Leruez, 1980). Recent difficulties lend weight to the view that 'indicative planning' enjoys apparent success only in expansionary times and simply gives some impetus to processes ultimately lying beyond the state's control. On the other hand it is likely that planned state investment in much needed infrastructure did much to launch France's successful post-war recovery.

In Britain, by contrast, comparable experiments were not given the time needed to test such theories. Thus, an ambitious national plan drawn up by an especially created Department of Economic Affairs, during Harold Wilson's 1964–6 government, was soon scrapped, together with the department itself. In practice, the Treasury success-fully reasserted its pre-eminent position in the economic policy-making domain. Equally, priority continued to be given to such established policies as the defence of sterling's international standing. The net result was, in effect, a continuance of existing 'stop-go' practices. Certainly efforts at comprehensive planning on the French model were abandoned and not resumed.

The abandonment of this experiment did not, however, mean an end to other more piecemeal or *ad hoc* extensions of state responsibility for economic affairs. Thus even Edward Heath's Conservative government, elected in 1970 with an initial commitment to scaling down state activity, was constrained to nationalize Rolls Royce rather than allow such a major national asset to go bankrupt. More significantly, Labour governments experimented with governmental agencies intended to foster the 'rationalization' of important industrial sectors and to promote mergers between enterprises deemed to be operating on an inefficiently small scale.

Of probably greater longer term political importance, however, were intrusions into certain areas which, at least in peace time, had generally been regarded as 'off limits' so far as the state was concerned. Thus, starting with Wilson's government of 1966–70, and continuing with more determination during Heath's 1970–4 govern-ment, serious attempts were made to regulate (through the use of the law) the relationships between private employers and their employees (Crouch, 1977). In face of continuing economic decline accompanied by increasingly evident inflationary pressures, and following disenchantment with ambitious planning ventures, there was a shift of emphasis towards placing limitations on collective bargaining and strike activity. Underlying the shift was the assumption that the problem of decline was, to a significant degree, associated with high wage costs and disorderly trade union practices. Thus the apparently perennial struggle of trade unions to preserve members' living standards and their existing differentials was seen as an economically destabilizing phenomenon that needed to be set within a constraining legal framework.

Threats to the unity of the labour movement led Wilson's government to abandon its initial venture in this sphere before legislation was enacted. The succeeding Conservative government, however, did pass an Industrial Relations Act but opposition from the trade union movement made it difficult if not impossible to enforce. Partly for that reason the same government sought to tackle the question of wage costs through the alternative medium of an official incomes policy. Trade union opposition to that policy, notably in the form of a miners' strike, eventually precipitated a major crisis that Edward Heath sought to resolve through a general election (in February 1974). The Labour party's return to power as a consequence of that election put paid to the endeavour. The subsequent government of James Callaghan (who succeeded Wilson as prime minister in 1976) renewed the attempt to run an incomes policy – a policy that was seen as a significant part of a general strategy for dealing with ever mounting inflation. It seems to be widely accepted that the troubled labour relations that accompanied this attempt played a large part in determining the outcome of the general election of May 1979 which brought Britain's present Conservative government into office. Clearly, therefore, these matters of industrial relations and of incomes policy became major if unresolved political dilemmas.

Another contentious matter during the 1970s was Britain's membership of the EEC (European Economic Community). Early applications to join the Community had been made in the 1960s, first by the Conservative government of Harold Macmillan and then by the post-1966 Labour government of Harold Wilson. Both of these applications can be regarded as a response to growing awareness of Britain's changed and diminishing world role. They may also be regarded as part of the same preoccupation with relative decline and the consequent need for 'modernization' that underlay European-inspired experiments in planning. De Gaulle's opposition, however, meant that entry into the Community was delayed until 1973 after Heath's government had finally obtained British membership. Nevertheless, formal entry did not definitively resolve the issue for, notably within the Labour party, vocal opposition to the whole venture persisted. On returning to office Harold Wilson sought to resolve this serious problem of internal party management by referring the matter to a national referendum. That referendum produced resounding support for continued membership but, in practice, this did not end the Labour party's debate. Indeed, withdrawal from the EEC became official party policy after 1979.

Of perhaps greater longer term importance, however, is the fact that membership has so far failed to yield the significant economic dividends anticipated by its earlier advocates. Rather, attention has been focussed on possible anomalies, notably the Common Agricultural Policy, which clearly work to Britain's disadvantage. Consequently, the institutions of the EEC have generally seemed unable to command sustained positive support from much of the British electorate. Equally, there is a significant body of opinion which sees continued membership as part of the national problem rather than a possible solution. Certainly, membership judged in terms of measurable economic returns can be seen as one of a series of new departures, all of which have so far not reversed the process of decline.

1.3 INTERPRETATIONS OF BRITAIN'S PROBLEMS

In the remainder of this chaper it is intended to identify factors, or dilemmas, of a largely political kind, that have been mooted by various schools of thought as possible explanations of Britain's basic problem. Such explanations or interpretations, it has to be stressed, are not necessarily mutually exclusive. In reality it seems likely that many factors are involved and certainly there is much room for debate about their respective significance. Indeed, as this discussion draws to its conclusion, some attention will be drawn to the conflicting diagnoses of and remedies for our contemporary economic ills that are currently on Britain's political agenda.

Commentators on Britain's economic problems have seen the chief difficulties as lying on a number of quite different levels of which we can perhaps note four. Firstly, there are those who emphasize the international context, the constraints this has imposed and the problems Britain has experienced in seeking to adjust to changes within in it (see Gamble, 1981). Some have suggested that Britain's problems are of very longstanding and stem (perhaps paradoxically) from the position that Britain came to occupy in the world, and the practices it espoused as a consequence of its early success as the first industrial nation. Such commentators stress that initial competitive advantages, reinforced by the acquisition of an empire and once pre-eminent sea power, gave Britain an early vested interest in free trading practices, practices that became part of the conventional wisdom of Britain's political and business leaders but which served the country less well once such powerful industrial competitors as Germany, the USA and, later, Japan moved decisively onto the international stage. Established British industries then became highly vulnerable to the competition of newcomers who, in some major instances, could rely on a degree of state protection and encouragement that in Britain had been precluded from the outset. Equally, it is suggested that Britain's economic headstart, and its accompanying power and prestige, for long masked the underlying vulnerability of its position. For example, the emergence of London as a great international financial centre perhaps gave an impression of economic strength that may have been belied by close examination of the country's basic manufacturing industries. Such industries, without immediate or obvious incentives to transform established practices, have long remained resistant to the changes ultimately needed to restore competitiveness.

As an extension of the same general argument, some would draw particular attention to recent but decisive changes in the terms or conditions of international trade, to which a trading nation with Britain's distinctive historical experience may be especially vulnerable. On this view, dependence on trade makes Britain particularly liable to the effects of inflationary pressures generated internationally. On a different plane, it could also be asserted that the emergence of the modern, foreign-owned, multi-national corporation poses fresh political challenges for a British state long wedded to a free trading othodoxy.

Similar commentators, focussing on a shorter time span, have stressed particular post-Second World War difficulties stemming from political attitudes or assumptions which first arose in association with Britain's great power status but which then persisted into an era of diminished status (Shonfield, 1958). Such critics particularly cite the arguably disproportionate costs associated with maintaining defence commitments and with defending the international position of sterling.

Secondly, another more sociological mode of analysis identified major domestic problems arising from long-term and extensive changes in British society, changes that may be associated with economic developments and have economic implications but which are as much social or political in character as economic. In particular attention has been drawn to problems of government and difficulties in official economic management that have stemmed from changing perceptions of authority or changing evaluations of Britain's class structures (for instance, see Goldthorpe, 1978).

Thus it is suggested that, despite post-war reforms, deep-seated inequalities of wealth, income and opportunity remain entrenched in

British society but that, by comparison with earlier periods, those at the apex of established hierarchies now command much less automatic deference within the wider community. The legitimacy of established inequalities has therefore become more questionable. Conversely, it is indicated, the working class, through its trade unions, has acquired an enhanced organizational capacity and increased awareness. This is not necessarily to imply the widespread embracing of clearly articulated socialist values. Indeed, the Conservative victories of 1979 and 1983 may in part have been due to a perception amongst some workers that a Conservative government might bring them increased prosperity. Rather it is to imply a greater assertiveness on the part of many groups in claiming an increased portion of society's material or other rewards.

Similarly, it has been argued that trade union bargaining and organization at the national level has led workers to evaluate their own economic position on the basis of less parochial and more wide-ranging comparisons (see Halsey, 1978). This too increased expectations and created a situation, not only of increased militancy vis-à-vis employers, but also of what amounted to competition within the Labour movement itself. It was such a situation that inspired governments to intervene in the sphere of industrial relations and to experiment with incomes policies. In so far as an accelerating scramble for increased wages was deemed to be a significant cause of inflation, governments felt it necessary to foster restraint in this area. Difficulties encountered on the way, however, suggested that in a climate of transformed expectations, the problem was deep-seated and, at least in the short run, not readily susceptible to governmental manipulation. Equally, the difficulties were symptomatic of a situation on the industrial relations front characterised by frequent mistrust in labour's dealings with management, a situation that some see as a major obstacle to successful industrial regeneration (for example, Fox, 1974).

An associated mode of analysis stresses the extent to which a scramble for resources of the type alluded to above, is necessarily bound up with the dynamics and the very nature of a free market economy operating on mainly capitalist principles. The latter's stress on competition and profit maximization tends ultimately to affect most social groups and, by the same token, to erode social relationships based on trust and co-operation. Ultimately, the stability of the market economy itself can be impeded by such developments for, perhaps paradoxically, the successful working of the market may partly depend on a degree of restraint and trust that may only come from the sharing of certain cultural and non-economic values (as suggested, for instance, in Hirsh, 1977). For example, the stability of the system presupposes the generally binding nature of contractual agreements. Commentators highlighting this issue argue that, in practice, the strivings of the market-place, and of the mass consumer society, may have contributed to a depletion of that reserve of shared cultural and even moral assumptions that might initially have facilitated the development of a capitalist system. In so far as the task of official economic management is complicated by changed popular expectations, such deep-seated cultural and social phenomena have clear political significance.

Thirdly, there are commentators with a more obviously political focus, who see problems in the dynamics and nature of Britain's party system (for example, Brittan, 1975). One view is that electoral competition has led parties, in their desire to outbid each other, to foster unrealistic economic expectations. In the scramble for votes and office, promises of prosperity are made that the economy is unable to realize. According to this analysis governments are forced to bridge the gap between income received from a limited tax base and growing public expenditure by extensive borrowing, or the printing of money with its dangerous inflationary consequences. Viewed from this perspective there is a need to modify or even reverse the expectations which politicians have previously helped to foster. Others, approaching the matter from a somewhat different angle, argue that the apparently adversarial quality of Britain's (until recently) two-party competition or debate has made for inconsistent and dramatically changing policy initiatives (see Finer, 1975). Alternating governments, and alternative policies, it is implied, impede balanced or sustained economic development because a climate of uncertainty surrounds the operations of the economy. One example of this is the abrupt changes of course in the sphere of industrial relations legislation. Such commentators tend to argue for electoral reform and a system of proportional representation that would facilitate the emergence of apparently more centrist coalition governments able to command wider public support than may now be the case and to ensure greater long-term continuity in policy-making. Other commentators, however, suggest that on close inspection the apparently adversarial nature of debate, with certain significant exceptions, tends to conceal a substantial degree of continuity in policy-making (Rose, 1980). These writers tend to stress the extent to which the mass electorate, as opposed to party activists, has shared certain values or assumptions and so constrained parties seeking its support, to avoid diametrically opposed positions. They suggest the existence of a substantial degree of consensus in British society to which the parties ultimately respond. Sometimes implicit in this approach is the view that the radical treatment which our economic ills may require is precluded by electoral constraints.

Not dissimilar views are expressed by exponents of a fourth approach who, focussing upon the institutions of the state itself, argue that within the policy-making domain the conventional party battle, though significant, tends to be overshadowed by regular dealings between the government and civil servants on the one hand and relevant interest groups on the other (Richardson and Jordon, 1979). The constant interchanges of the state officials and group spokesmen constitute a mainspring of the policy-making process. By the same token the dependence of governments upon the goodwill of groups for the identification of problems as well as for the formulation and execution of appropriate policy responses means, according to this interpretation, that the state has only limited freedom of manoeuvre. The state, viewed from this perspective, is so constrained or hemmed in by complex networks of relationships with highly organized interests, that much continuity is necessarily maintained and most policy-making goes on within predictable boundaries. Indeed, the multiplicity of groups (alluded to earlier in this discussion) which seek state action now make such wide-ranging demands that a debate has sprung up concerning the so called 'overloading' of modern industrial states (see for example, Rose, 1980). In the particular case of Britain, such problems may be exacerbated by the existence of a civil service, of nineteenth-century origins, whose traditions, interests, and outlook do not equip it well for governmental tasks of such a complex and frequently technical variety. (This is implied by Heclo and Wildavsky, 1974.)

One influential interpretation of the issues at stake has argued that the British state (along with others) has moved in the direction of 'corporatism' (see Winkler and Pahl, 1975; Harrison, 1980; and Middlemas, 1979). Thus the state has been constrained to make policy in conjunction with major interests (most notably business and trade unions) whose spokesmen have been incorporated, on a regular basis, into decision-making processes. Political developments during the 1970s in particular are interpreted in these terms.

1.4 CURRENT DEBATES

In the early 1980s British political debate reflects the existence of sharply contrasting responses to all these dilemmas and to the failure of successive governments to wrestle successfully with chronic economic difficulties. Perhaps three major responses can here be identified. Firstly, there is the view, represented by the present government's principal economic policy-makers that the answer to our problems ultimately lies in a decisive shift away from state economic management and back toward more traditional forms of relatively untrammelled free market competition. Thus not only are established free trading othodoxies embraced, but this view holds that industrial regeneration is only likely to come as a consequence of the incentives or disciplines supplied by the free play of market forces (on the latter, see Friedman, 1962, and Hayek, 1944). Thus parts of the public sector are to be sold off. Equally, it is maintained, recovery cannot come if resources are channelled into the public sector and away from productive investment in the private sector. Public expenditure, in other words, has, in the long term, to be cut. Similarly, strict controls should be applied to the supply of money and to the size of state borrowing in order to contain inflationary pressures. Indeed, the curbing of inflation has been given clear priority over such other post-war aims of official policy as the curbing of unemployment.

Unemployment is certainly not a purely British phenomenon. It is a widespread feature of an international economic recession. However, its existence in Britain on its present scale seems to be accepted, within this ideological framework, as a necessary price to pay for the achievement of long-term goals. Not least, it is at least implicitly assumed that it should foster a general climate of diminishing mass economic expectations constraining trade unions to moderate wage demands. In other words, such a climate, together with fresh industrial relations legislation, is expected to diminish the allegedly excessive bargaining power of organized labour – power which, it is deemed, has inflationary consequences and interferes with the smooth workings of the market.

Within the Conservative party the ascendancy of such classic liberal notions represents a novel departure (a departure made possible by disillusionment with the results of post-war Conservative attempts to manage the economy). It is at odds with traditional Conservative approaches to the use of state power. It is also at odds with that traditional Conservative pragmatism which generally declines to adopt fixed ideological positions. However, exponents of more traditional Conservative approaches remain to pursue an internal party debate whose final outcome remains unknown. They (together with representatives of other political traditions) are afraid that strict adherence to monetarist orthodoxies could accelerate rather than halt industrial decline. It is feared that an absence of public investment, private business confidence and effective consumer demand could cause irreversible damage to productive capacity. It is further feared that official policies may not so much reverse as frustrate popular expectations and so create public disorder (of the sort already witnessed, in inner cities, during 1981) or inadvertently strengthen radical forces of the Left.

A second major response to current problems is represented by the Labour party's 'Alternative Strategy', an intellectual basis for which is provided in Holland (1975). This strategy also marks a departure in a different direction from post-war political orthodoxies. Thus it advocates, at least temporarily, the abandonment of free trading traditions and the pursuit of industrial regeneration behind protective tariff walls; withdrawal from the EEC is seen as part of this exercise. It also envisages an unprecedented planning role for the state. Finally, rather than perceiving a need to diminish organized labour's bargaining power it advocates popular participation in decision-making, at all levels of the economic and political system, and a major redistribution of wealth in favour of the working class. Earlier corporatist arrangements are seen as involving unduly restricted elite groups as being underpinned, within society at large, by insufficiently democratic industrial relations. Long-term economic stability and productivity, it is suggested, depends on the creation of economic and political institutions with a higher degree of accountability and acceptability than is currently the case. Instead of seeking radically to diminish the state's economic role in favour of greater free market competition the accent here is upon a more radical use of the state than hitherto, in order to diminish inequalities associated with the market.

Critics of this approach are doubtful about Britain's capacity successfully to extricate itself from existing international economic entanglements. Not least, it is feared that protectionist measures will invite retaliation from rivals so that more markets will be definitively lost. Equally, doubts are expressed about the economic costs and political tensions likely, at least in the short run, to arise from attempts at radical social engineering. It is feared, for example, that private industry would cease to invest, there would be a dramatic flight of capital abroad and that substantial popular support could be mobilized by threatened interests so that potentially destabilizing political polarization could conceivably ensue.

Such anxieties are to some degree shared by advocates of a third broad set of responses to current dilemmas. They reject the above radical models, of both Right and Left, in favour of a continued if significantly modified consensual approach (as expressed, for instance, in Owen, 1981, and Williams, 1981). In doing so they note the undoubted erosion of the post-war 'Butskellite' consensus and seek to supply a political formula which could fill the resulting vacuum. They can point to recent moves away from established Keynesian forms of economic management (first observable under Labour rule but much more evident under the present government). They also note the possibility of attacks on the welfare state. On the more obviously political plane they further note an evident long-term decline in support for the established political parties and an accompanying tendency for the electorate to be more volatile which, in the 1970s, resulted in relatively frequent changes of government. Not least they point to the demands of Scottish and Welsh Nationalists, to the suspicions of central government these indicate and to the question mark against the United Kingdom's unity that they may represent. Most fundamentally they perceive that such difficulties, in large measure, signify disenchantment with the apparent inability of successive governments successfully to grapple with long-term economic problems. Their response is not to try and decisively shift the balance of advantages in favour of capital or labour nor to abandon the mixed economy but to build broad-based support, if possible, across class lines, for a widely acceptable reform programme – a programme that would seek to restore faith in political institutions and so make them more effective engineers of economic change. Electoral reform and regional devolution are amongst the relevant changes that are mooted. The pursuit of an incomes policy is another feature of the programme. Such changes are particularly identified with the new Social Democratic Party, and its Liberal Party ally, but elements of the same thinking are also to be found in the two other British political parties.

At present, great uncertainty surrounds the efforts of those concerned to re-fashion such a consensus in British society. This is part of a wider uncertainty about the future of the political system and its capacity to handle perennial economic dilemmas. The next few years will therefore see a continuing debate within and between the parties concerning the issues raised in this chapter and the appropriate economic policies to pursue.

Students of the British economy will certainly not be able to ignore the political context within which it operates.

REFERENCES

Addison, P. (1975) *The Road to 1945* (London: Cape).

Beer, S. H. (1969) *Modern British Politics*, 2nd ed. (London: Faber).

Brittan, S. (1964) *The Treasury under the Tories* (Harmondsworth: Penguin).

Brittan, S. (1975) 'The Economic Contradictions of Democracy', *British Journal of Political Science*, vol. 5 (2), April, pp. 129–160.

Crosland, C. A. R. (1964) *The Future of Socialism* (London: Cape).

Crouch, C. (1977) *Class Conflict and the Industrial Relations Crisis* (London: Heinemann).

Finer, S. E. (ed.) (1975) *Adversary Politics and Electoral Reform* (London: Wigram).

Fox, A. (1974) *Beyond Contract: Work, Power and Trust Relations* (London: Faber).

Friedman, M. (1962) *Capitalism and Freedom* (Chicago: University of Chicago Press).

Gamble, A. (1981) *Britain in Decline* (London: Macmillan).

Goldthorpe, J. H. (1978) 'The Current Inflation: Towards a Sociological Explanation', in F. Hirsh and J. H. Goldthorpe (eds.), *The Political Economy of Inflation* (London: Martin Robertson).

Halsey, A. H. (1978) *Change in British Society* (Oxford: Oxford University Press).

Harrison, R. J. (1980) *Pluralism and Corporatism* (London: Allen & Unwin).

Hayek, F. A. (1944) *The Road to Serfdom* (London: Routledge).

Heclo, H. and Wildavsky, A. (1974) *The Private Government of Public Money* (London: Macmillan).

Holland, S. (1975) *The Socialist Challenge* (London: Quartet Books).

Leruez, J. (1980) 'Planning in an Overloaded Economy', in R. Rose (ed.) (1980) *Challenge to Governance: Studies in Overload Politics* (London: Sage).

Marwick, A. (1968) *Britain in the Century of Total War* (London: Bodley Head).

Middlemas, K. (1979) *Politics in Industrial Society: The Experience of the British Political System since 1911* (London: Andre Deutsch).

Minkin, L. (1978) *The Labour Party Conference* (London: Allen Lane).

Owen, D. (1981) *Face the Future* (London: Cape).

Richardson, J. J. and Jordan, A. G. (1979) *Governing under Pressure: The Policy Process in a Post-Parliamentary Democracy* (Oxford: Martin Robertson).

Rose, R. (1980) *Do Parties Make a Difference?* (London: Macmillan).

Shonfield, A. (1958) *British Economic Policy since the War* (Harmondsworth: Penguin Books).

Shonfield, A. (1976) *Modern Capitalism: the Changing Balance of Public and Private Power* (Oxford: Oxford University Press).

Williams, R. (1971) *Politics and Technology* (London: Macmillan).

Williams, S. (1981) *Politics is for People* (Harmondsworth: Penguin Books).

Winkler, J. J. and Pahl, R. (1975) 'The Coming Corporatism', *Challenge*, March–April.

QUESTIONS FOR DISCUSSION

1   Do you think that improved British economic performance demands less or more state intervention in economic life?

2   To what extent, if at all, have Britain's recent economic problems

been due to 'excessive material expectations' on the part of the electorate. To what extent have politicians been responsible for stimulating such expectations?

3 To what extent has declining economic performance been due to the existence of inefficient or outmoded governmental and political institutions?

4 Do you think it is possible or desirable to re-establish the type of political 'consensus' that apparently characterized British politics after 1945?

5 Does British membership of the EEC offer a long-term solution to this country's economic difficulties?

6 'The politics of scarcity' – to what extent does this phrase illuminate the present state of British political debate?

7 How useful is the notion of 'corporatism' in helping us to understand British politics during the 1970s?

8 Would a coalition government offer a ready solution to Britain's economic difficulties?

SUGGESTED READING

The debates alluded to above can be pursued with the aid of any good newspaper. *The Financial Times* is particularly recommended for many of the issues. *The Economist* produces briefing papers on political matters that may be helpful. Finally, attention is drawn to R. Crossman, *The Crossman Diaries*, ed. Anthony Howard (Methuen, 1979). L. Chapman, *Your Disobedient Servant* (Penguin, 1979). C. Hood and M. Wright (eds.) *Big Government in Hard Times* (Oxford: Martin Robertson 1979).

Part I
MACROECONOMIC POLICY

2 The Overall Management of the Economy[1]

C. V. BROWN

My purpose is to explain some of the controversy that surrounds the macroeconomic policy of the present Conservative government. The government attaches the highest importance to the reduction of inflation, claiming that until inflation is reduced it is impossible to reduce unemployment – except perhaps temporarily and at the cost of more inflation later. The critics of the government on the other hand argue that unemployment could be reduced with only a modest increase in inflation. If these critics are correct, not only are the unemployed suffering unnecessarily, but the whole economy is worse off by the amount that those who are unemployed could have produced. As unemployment is now over three million, or one in eight of the labour force, this potential loss of output is very large.

While the debate is almost never expressed in these terms, it is to a considerable extent a debate about how elastic aggregate supply is.[2] If the aggregate supply curve is highly elastic, like AS_1 in Figure 2.1, an increase in aggregate demand will raise output but not prices. On the other hand, if aggregate supply is highly inelastic, like AS_2 in Figure 2.1, an increase in demand will increase prices not output. I propose to devote this chapter to a discussion of aggregate supply, the factors affecting its elasticity and the policy implications of alternative elasticities. Throughout I have assumed a closed economy (one without international trade). This is clearly unrealistic for the British economy, but is a useful starting point: the effects of openness are considered most fully in Chapter 6.

2.1 CAPACITY OUTPUT

The capacity of the economy to produce is determined by the

available stocks of factors such as land, labour and capital. The total stock of land will change only *very* slowly through time, but of course it is possible to change the way that land is used more quickly and thus to increase its productivity. The stock of labour available for work will depend on the total population; its age structure; the conventions or laws about education and retirement; and the proportion of people who wish to work at current wage rates. The capital stock depends on how much net investment there has been in the past. For each of these factors quality taken individually is important. The amount that can be produced by any given capital stock depends on the technology embodied in that stock. In addition, the capacity of the economy depends on how well the stocks of factors are combined together. Thus if the skills embodied in the labour force are not properly matched to the skills needed to operate the capital stock, output will be lower than if the fit is good. Finally, the factors must be capable of producing the range of goods that people wish to buy.

In the short run the total capacity of the economy may or may not be reached. If factors of production are well matched to each other and to the mix of goods people wish to buy, we can concentrate on any one factor and it is conventional to concentrate on labour. If factors are well matched to each other, all factors of production will be fully employed when everyone is able to do as much work as they wish to at the current wage rates.[3] This does *not* imply that everyone is working, far less that everyone is working twenty-four hours a day, since some people will not wish to work at all and others will only wish to work part time, because, for example, they have children or other dependents to care for. Other people may wish to leave the labour market temporarily either because a seasonal pattern of working suits them or because they wish to spend time improving their qualifications.

One of our objectives must be to explain why it is that some people may be involuntarily unemployed; that is, why they are unable to find work at current wage rates. Is this involuntary unemployment somehow related to wages or the price level? To see how it might be, let us look more closely at short-run supply curves for the whole economy such as those shown in Figure 2.1. Figure 2.1 has both output and employment on the horizontal axes. This is simplifying slightly for it assumes that output increases proportionately to employment, when in fact output probably increases less rapidly than employment due to diminishing returns to the employment of additional units of labour. There is a vertical line representing the capacity level of output which is determined by the factors mentioned above. The vertical axis shows some measure of the average level of prices such as the retail price index. The short-run aggregate supply curve shows the amounts of output that producers are willing to

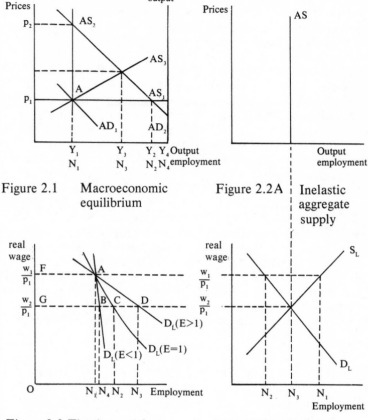

Figure 2.1   Macroeconomic equilibrium

Figure 2.2A   Inelastic aggregate supply

Figure 2.3 The demand for labour

Figure 2.2B Equilibrium in the labour market

produce at various prices. The shape of this curve is critical for the debate between the government and its critics.

Suppose that we happen to be at point A in Figure 2.1 where there is considerable unemployment ($= N_4 - N_1$) and where output is below capacity by $Y_4 - Y_1$. The average price level is P_1. The aggregate demand curve[4] AD_1 passes through A. Suppose that we now increase the level of aggregate demand to AD_2. What will happen to unemployment and to prices? It can be seen from Figure 2.1 that the answer depends on the aggregate supply curve. If the aggregate supply curve were the perfectly elastic (that is, horizontal) AS_1 the government's critics would be correct and we could raise employment from N_1 to N_2 and leave the price level at P_1. On the other hand, if the aggregate supply curve were the perfectly inelastic (that is, vertical) AS_2, raising aggregate demand to AD_2 would raise prices to P_2 without affecting either output or employment.

Clearly these two extremes do not exhaust the possibilities. Thus, if the elasticity of the aggregate supply curve lies between zero and infinity, an increase in aggregate demand will raise output and employment as well as prices. This possibility may be represented by the aggregate supply curve AS_3 and it can be seen that an increase in aggregate demand to AD_2 causes output and employment to rise to Y_3 and N_3 respectively and prices to rise to P_3. It can thus be seen that the elasticity of the aggregate supply curve shows us the trade-off between unemployment and price levels. If the elasticity is low and AS_3 were quite close to AS_2, an increase in demand would have a large impact on prices and very little impact on unemployment. On the other hand, if the elasticity of aggregate supply is high and AS_3 lies quite close to AS_1 an increase in aggregate demand will reduce unemployment substantially with only a minimal effect on prices. It is thus clear that knowledge of the elasticity of supply is critical if we are to be able to choose between the economic policies of the government and its critics. Economists have had a number of rather different ideas about the elasticity of aggregate supply and I will now explain some of these.

2.2 VIEWS ABOUT THE ELASTICITY OF SUPPLY

The classical view[5]
The classical or pre-Keynesian economists viewed the aggregate supply curve as totally inelastic. They reached this conclusion from their analysis of the labour market. They believed, for reasons that should be familiar from introductory microeconomics, that the demand curve for labour would be downwards sloping, meaning that producers would wish to hire more labour when its price (that is, the wage rate) was low. The supply curve for labour was upwards sloping, implying that more people would wish to work at high-wage rates than at low-wage rates. This view of the labour market is represented in Figure 2.2B which has employment on the horizontal axis and the real wage, that is money wages divided by an index of consumer prices, on the vertical axis. The classical view of the labour market was that it behaved like any other competitive market with the price, in this case the real wage rate, being determined by the interaction of supply and demand. If the current wage rate happened to be W_1/P_1 then N_1

workers would wish to work but producers would only wish to hire N_2 workers so there would be unemployment of N_1 - N_2. However, this unemployment would be temporary for some of the unemployed workers would offer to work for a money wage below W_1 and so the money wage could fall until the real wage was W_2/P_1, assuming that the price level also did not fall. Unemployment was thus a temporary phenomenon and employment would tend to stabilize at the equilibrium level of N_3.

It should be noted that N_3 represents full employment because everyone who wishes to work at the equilibrium wage rate of W_2/P_1 is able to do so. If, minor aberrations aside, full employment was assured, then this would also determine the level of output. With the existing capital stock, state of technology, quality of labour, etc., N_3 workers could produce some particular level of output. This level of output is shown in Part A of Figure 2.2 where the two parts of the figure have the same scale on the horizontal axis. The classical economists thus expected a vertical aggregate supply curve. In these circumstances, it has been shown (see Figure 2.1) that a change in aggregate demand will only affect prices, and not output.[6]

Keynes's views

Keynes thought this view of the classical economists was fundamentally mistaken for a variety of reasons, but perhaps most importantly because it neglected the principle of effective demand. Keynes spent a whole chapter (19) in his *General Theory* arguing that cuts in money wages would not necessarily restore full employment. He suggested that producers will only hire labour if they expect to be able to sell the goods produced by that labour, and that requires an adequate level of aggregate demand. Critical to his argument is the behaviour of personal consumption where Keynes argued that workers will wish to spend part, but not all, of any change in their income on consumption. If the other elements of aggregate demand are constant and if workers' income falls, they will reduce their consumption which means that there will be an equal fall in aggregate demand. The reduction in aggregate demand will reduce and possibly reverse the expansionary effects of cuts in money wages.

Keynes of the introductory textbook

Most analysis that takes account of aggregate supply curves is omitted from introductory (and many intermediate) textbooks. Instead there is the familiar Keynesian cross in which the equilibrium level of income is determined by the interaction of the total expenditure function (E = C + I) and the 45° line. How does this conventional analysis relate to our present discussion, which is focussing on the elasticity of the aggregate supply curve? The assumption is made (often implicitly) that up to the level of capacity output the aggregate supply curve is perfectly elastic, and that it becomes perfectly inelastic when capacity output is reached. If the aggregate supply curve is perfectly elastic when output is below capacity, unemployment can be eliminated by an expansion of aggregate demand without price increases.[7] This is equivalent to a shift in the aggregate demand curve from AD_1 to AD_2 in Figure 2.1. This implicit perfectly elastic segment of the aggregate supply curve explains why most introductory textbooks have the greatest difficulty in explaining how inflation can coexist with unemployment.

Keynes of the General Theory

While models which at least implicitly assume a perfectly elastic segment to the aggregate supply curve are presented as the standard Keynesian model, this analysis is clearly and explicitly rejected by Keynes himself who believed that the aggregate supply curve would be upward sloping.[8] Some of the reasons Keynes advanced for this are as follows.

1. As unemployment falls the additional workers hired are likely to be paid the same wage as existing workers but may be less efficient so costs of production will rise.
2. As unemployment falls less efficient capital equipment will need to be brought into production and this will increase unit costs further.
3. There are likely to be shortages or bottlenecks of some factors while others are still abundant. Once these bottlenecks are reached, there is likely to be a 'sharp rise' in some prices.
4. When output in certain sectors expands ahead of the general increase in output, employers of these groups of workers will be more likely to grant wage increases.

The strength of all these factors will probably increase in importance as full employment is approached. Thus Keynes's own view of the shape of the aggregate supply curve is as shown in Figure 2.4A. Starting from some low level of aggregate demand such as AD_1 it is possible to expand demand to AD_2, achieving a relatively large increase in output and employment in exchange for a relatively modest increase in prices. However, as full employment capacity output is approached, higher levels of employment can only be 'bought' at increasingly severe penalties in terms of the price level as can be seen from the comparison of AD_3 and AD_4.

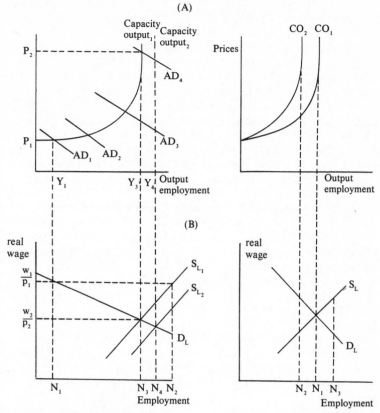

Figure 2.4 Anticipated and
          unanticipated
          inflation

Figure 2.5 Structural
          unemployment

Expectations

Recently arguments have been advanced which suggest that expectations about inflation are an important element in the explanation of the trade-off between unemployment and inflation. It will be easier to see this if we first relate the discussion of Keynes's aggregate supply curve in 2.4A to what is happening in the labour market as shown in 2.4B. When the level of aggregate demand is low at AD_1 in Figure 2.4A, the real wage in Figure 2.4B is high at W_1/P_1 and the demand for labour is low at N_1. At this real wage the supply of labour is N_2 and unemployment is $N_2 - N_1$. As aggregate demand is increased, money wages are bid up in those sectors where bottlenecks first arise, but prices rise more than money wages because of the lower efficiency of new workers, bringing into use older machines, etc. Because prices rise faster than money wages, real wages must fall. Employment rises to N_3 and unemployment is eliminated.

It has been suggested that the above argument requires modification if inflation is not anticipated. Let us suppose that there has been a long period of stable or falling prices (as occurred in Britain between the two world wars). People have come to expect stable prices. Let us further suppose that the supply curve of labour in Figure 2.4B represents the supply curve when inflation is correctly anticipated. If so, what happens if people expect no price increases but they nevertheless occur? We have seen that as full employment approaches, money wages will rise. If people who have received a higher money wage do not expect prices to rise, they will believe that their real wage has risen. With a positively sloped labour supply curve, people will wish to supply more labour at (what they believe to be) this higher real wage. They will attempt to move up the supply curve AS_1. However prices are in fact rising which means that the supply curve has shifted to the right to S_{L2}. S_{L1} is thus the supply curve when the expected change in prices equals the actual change in prices, whereas S_{L2} is the supply curve when the expected change in prices is less than the actual change in prices or is zero. The effect of workers persistently failing to anticipate inflation is that the full employment levels of employment and output rise from N_3 and Y_3 to N_4 and Y_4.

Many economists believe that a mechanism rather like this explains why it was possible for Britain and other countries to operate at *very* low levels of unemployment for the first couple of decades after the Second World War. During that period inflation was initially very low but it gradually rose, and as it rose workers came increasingly to anticipate inflation. Once inflation is fully anticipated the distinction between S_1 and S_2 in 2.4B disappears as S_2 merges back into S_1 and capacity output is effectively reduced from CO_2 to CO_1.

The implication of this argument is that we may not be able to repeat the success of the fifties and early sixties of combining low levels of inflation with low levels of unemployment now that inflation is more or less fully anticipated.

There are other arguments that point in the same direction, all of which tend to suggest that even though unemployment is now high, the elasticity of the aggregate supply curve may be low.

Frictional unemployment and redundancy pay

When workers are made redundant, they have been entitled, since the mid-sixties, to more generous redundancy pay than in the past, in addition to unemployment pay or supplementary benefits. Although there is no conclusive evidence to support this, it is argued that more generous financial treatment will mean that a worker may be less likely to accept a new job hurriedly, especially if the job itself or the pay are less attractive than in the former job. Thus redundancy payments are among the factors affecting frictional unemployment, of which there is further discussion in the next chapter.

Structural unemployment

It was assumed at the start of this chapter that labour and capital were reasonably well matched to each other. Suppose, however, that the pattern of demand is changing and people want more specialised services, more electronic goods and rather less from heavy industry. As coal mining, steel production, ship building, etc., contract, labour will be released that is likely to be in the wrong place and to have the wrong skills to meet expanded demand for accountants, local government officers, computer programmers, and so on.

The classical economists were able to sweep this problem under the carpet because of their assumption of perfect labour markets. If some skills were surplus and others in short supply, wages would fall in the surplus skill categories and would rise where there were shortages. This change in relative wages would cause workers to move from labour surplus areas to labour shortage areas and was part of the argument that unemployment would be temporary as it would be eliminated by changes in relative wages.

Labour markets are clearly not perfectly competitive in practice. Large unions bargain nationally for wages which are then expected to apply both in areas of labour surplus and labour shortage. In addition, there are conventional wage hierarchies both between skill levels in particular industries and between different types of workers. So long as these wage hierarchies are maintained they prevent changes in relative wages and will tend to perpetuate structural unemployment.

The very fast pace of technological change may also increase structural unemployment because technological change brings both new products and new techniques for producing both old and new products. Most people stop their formal training four or five decades before they retire and when change is rapid, it is not surprising that people's skills become out of date.

When there is structural unemployment there is a mismatch between labour and capital. Capacity output is reduced by whatever could have been produced by the structurally unemployed if this mismatch did not occur, and the aggregate supply curve also becomes less elastic. In the absence of structural unemployment, N_1 would represent the full employment level in Figure 2.5B and in 2.5A the corresponding capacity output is CO_1. With structural unemployment of $N_3 - N_2$, capacity output is reduced to CO_2 and then the aggregate supply curve becomes less elastic.

If it is correct that structural unemployment in Britain has risen, and the aggregate supply curve has become less elastic, then attempts to reduce unemployment by increasing aggregate demand will tend to increase inflation without reducing unemployment very much. There is more discussion of structural unemployment in the next chapter.

2.3 POLICY IMPLICATIONS

How does our discussion of the elasticity of aggregate supply affect the debate between the government and its critics? The reader will now recognize that a relevant question is 'How elastic is the aggregate supply curve?' No definitive answer to this question is possible but it may be worth ending with some speculations on this vital point. This will enable us to see if government policy is misguided. I think it is naive to imagine that we can reduce unemployment drastically and quickly by demand management alone. To this extent the government is probably on quite firm ground. It may well be the case that even with 3 million unemployed there is only a relatively small part of the aggregate supply curve which has a sufficiently high elasticity to make it possible to reduce unemployment easily. All too soon we would reach shortages of particular skills needed by particular industries (structural unemployment), and we would find that additional capital stock was required. That does *not* however imply that we must live with 2.5–3 million unemployed for the foreseeable future. What it does mean is that we have to attempt to deal with structural unemployment by regional policies, by retraining, and trying to introduce more flexibility into relative wage rates. If this is accompanied by a modest expansion of demand each year, it will provide business with the possibility of a much needed increase in profitability. If simultaneously interest rates are lowered this should increase the inducement to invest in both machines and in men, reducing both bottlenecks and structural unemployment. In this way, we can gradually increase the aggregate supply elasticity, as equilibrium output itself steadily expands.

The other important implication is that we can attempt to shift the aggregate supply curve down and to the right. This means being able to produce output at lower cost by becoming more efficient, and is important both domestically and from the point of view of improving Britain's performance in overseas markets.

I leave the last word with Keynes, who wrote as follows forty-six years ago:

It is natural to interject that it is premature to abate our efforts to increase employment so long as the figures of unemployment remain so large. In a sense this must be true. But I believe that we are approaching, or have reached, the point where there is not much advantage in applying a further general stimulus at the centre. So long as surplus resourses were widely diffused between industries and localities it was no great matter at what point in the economic structure the impulse of an increased demand was applied. But the evidence grows that – for several reasons into which there is no space to enter here – the economic structure is unfortunately rigid, and that (for example) building activity in the home counties is less effective than one might have hoped in decreasing unemployment in the distressed areas. It follows that the later stages of recovery require a different technique. To remedy the condition of the distressed areas, *ad hoc* measures are necessary.

What is required at once are acts of constructive imagination by our administrators, engineers, and achitects, to be followed by financial criticism, sifting, and more detailed designing; so that some large and useful projects, at least, can be launched at a few months' notice.

There can be no justification for a rate of interest which impedes an adequate flow of new projects at a time when the national resources for production are not fully employed. The rate of interest must be reduced to the figure that the new projects can afford. In special cases subsidies may be justified; but in general it is the long-term rate of interest which should come down to the figure which the marginal project can earn. *The Times*, 1937

NOTES

1   A fuller version of the argument set out in this chapter will be found in Brown (1984).
2   In general, an elasticity is the percentage change in a quantity or volume, divided by the percentage change in the corresponding price or income. In this case, therefore, we are interested in the responsiveness of aggregate supply (that is, the volume of goods and services firms are willing to produce in a given period, say a year) to changes in the overall price level.
3   In the section on structural unemployment (below) this assumption is dropped.
4   Aggregate demand is the sum of consumers' expenditure, investment

and government expenditure (in an open economy, we should also add exports and deduct imports). The aggregate demand curve shows the relation between aggregate demand and the price level, demand being determined by the condition that planned withdrawals and injections are equal.

5   The classical view was actually a good deal more complex than the conventional textbook account presented here.

6   This is an important part of the explanation for the quantity theory of money which postulated that $MV = PY$ where M is the stock of money, V the income velocity of circulation, P the average price level and Y the level of income. With full employment being assured and the aggregate supply completely inelastic, Y in the equation is fixed. The classical economists also believed that V was fixed and in these circumstances any change in M would bring forth an equal proportionate change in P.

7   'Thus if there is perfectly elastic supply so long as there is unemployment, and perfectly inelastic supply so soon as full employment is reached, and if effective demand changes in the same proportion as the quantity of money, the Quantity Theory of Money can be enunciated as follows: "So long as there is unemployment, *employment* will change in the same proportion as the quantity of money, and when there is full employment *prices* will change in the same proportion as the quantity of money" ' (*General Theory*, pp. 295–6)

8   'Thus instead of constant prices in conditions of unemployment ... we have in fact a condition of prices rising gradually as employment increases.' (*General Theory*, p. 296)

FURTHER READING

Brown, C. V. (1984) *Unemployment and Inflation: An Introduction to Macroeconomics* (Oxford: Martin Robertson), forthcoming.

Cairncross, Sir Alec (1981) 'Two Years without Cheers', *The Three Banks Review*, March.

Keynes, J. M. (1936) *The General Theory of Employment, Interest and Money* (London: Macmillan).

Meade, J. (1983) 'A New Keynesian Approach to Full Employment', *Lloyds Bank Review*, October.

Shackleton, J. R. (1982) 'Economists and Unemployment', *National Westminster Bank Quarterly Review*, February.

Thirwall, A. P. (1981) 'Keynesian Employment Theory is not Defunct', *The Three Banks Review*, September.

QUESTIONS FOR DISCUSSION

1   Why is knowledge of aggregate supply important?

2   Does net investment affect aggregate demand, aggregate supply

or both?
3   How do classical and Keynesian views differ as to the effect of an increase in demand on prices and unemployment?
4   The present government came to office in 1979 and pledged to reduce both government spending and taxation. Both have gone up. Why?

3 Unemployment

PAUL HARE

3.1 DEFINITION AND MEASUREMENT

Unemployment is usually defined as the difference between the number of people willing and able to work at prevailing wage rates, and those who actually have jobs. This difference is divided by the labour force to obtain the unemployment rate.

Unemployment in Britain has traditionally been measured as the number of people registered as unemployed at job centres on a particular day each month; since 1982 the measure used has been the number of people claiming benefit at Unemployment benefit offices each month. The General Household Survey shows that these measures consistently underestimate the true unemployment rate, in that some unemployed people (about 20 per cent) do not register either because they judge the chances of finding work to be very low (a factor which should be distinguished from their willingness to work), or more likely because their entitlement to unemployment benefit is non-existent or extinguished.

Job centres also record vacancies, but here the inaccuracy in the official figures is much greater. Surveys suggest that only about a third of vacancies are notified to the centres, the proportion being higher at times of high unemployment like the present, presumably because employers judge that the pool of unemployed is then more likely to include the workers they need.

Having indicated how unemployment is measured, one might expect that we should regard full employment quite simply as that state of the economy where measured unemployment is zero (making suitable allowance for those who do not register, of course). However, that is not normally the case, except in certain very simple theoretical models of the economy. In order to understand why not, it is helpful to distinguish between different types of unemployment. The most useful classification is in terms of the following categories:

   (i)   seasonal
  (ii)   structural
 (iii)   frictional
 (iv)   demand deficient.

Seasonal unemployment arises in a variety of occupations where production is difficult at certain times of the year (for example, construction), or where the nature of the work imposes different demands at different times (for example, agriculture). In addition, the demand for some products, especially services such as holiday accommodation in tourist resorts, is highly seasonal, and the pattern of employment in such trades tends to reflect this situation. Thus even in an ideally functioning economy, we would expect the level of employment (and hence unemployment) to fluctuate seasonally. For this reason, it is quite common for published figures on unemployment to be seasonally adjusted, to remove the effects of these fluctuations.

Aside from seasonal factors, unemployment rates are not the same in all areas and for all groups of the population. Certain areas have experienced persistently high rates compared with the average for Britain as a whole; and certain groups of the population suffer higher average rates as well as more frequent spells of unemployment. Thus the incidence of unemployment is far from uniform over the population. Consequently, a policy that results in unemployment inevitably imposes relatively high costs on a fairly small proportion of the population; some implications of this problem, and recent policy responses to it, are examined in Chapter 9, below.

Persistently higher unemployment rates in some regions or affecting certain occupations are often considered to represent *structural unemployment*. This occurs when industries which predominate in some region or regions begin to decline, and are not quickly replaced by newer, incoming industries. Thus the change in the regional distribution of production in the economy can give rise to pockets or even whole areas of relatively high unemployment. Similarly, a change in the pattern of jobs, perhaps due to mechanization or some other form of innovation, can make some skills totally redundant. Again, therefore, this can give rise to structural unemployment. Rigidities in relative wages often mean that such imbalances can persist for a very long time; at the regional level, the outmigration of some groups (often the more skilled) and the national determination of relative wages make adjustment more difficult than it might otherwise be. The persistence of structural unemployment, more or less irrespective of the general level of demand in the economy, explains why governments have so often sought to moderate its impact through a variety of policy measures, such as regional policy, protection of

Table 3.1   Regional unemployment rates

	1967	1971	1975	1976	1977	1978	1979	1980	1981	1982[a]
United Kingdom	2.3	3.5	4.1	5.7	6.2	6.1	5.8	7.4	11.3	13.8
North	3.9	5.7	5.9	7.4	8.3	8.8	8.6	10.9	15.0	17.6
Yorkshire and Humberside	1.9	3.8	4.0	5.6	5.8	6.0	5.7	7.8	12.1	14.6
East Midlands	1.6	2.9	3.6	4.7	5.0	5.0	4.7	6.4	10.1	12.1
East Anglia	2.0	3.2	3.4	4.8	5.3	5.0	4.5	5.7	9.1	11.2
South East	1.6	2.0	2.8	4.2	4.5	4.2	3.7	4.8	8.0	10.4
South West	2.5	3.3	4.7	6.3	6.8	6.5	5.7	6.7	9.9	11.8
West Midlands	1.8	2.9	4.1	5.8	5.8	5.6	5.5	7.8	13.5	16.6
North West	2.3	3.9	5.3	7.0	7.4	7.5	7.1	9.3	13.7	16.6
England	2.0	3.0	3.9	5.4	5.7	5.6	5.2	6.8	10.8	13.2
Wales	4.0	4.4	5.6	7.2	8.0	8.4	8.0	10.3	14.5	17.4
Scotland	3.7	5.8	5.2	6.9	8.1	8.2	8.0	10.0	13.6	15.8
Northern Ireland	7.3	7.9	7.9	10.0	11.0	11.5	11.3	13.7	18.3	21.7

Note: (a) October figure; other figures represent the average rate for the year in question.

SOURCES: Regional Trends 1981, p. 94. Employment Gazette, March 1982, Table 2.3. Regional Trends 1983, p. 85.

declining industries to slow down the rate of adjustment, efforts by the public sector to favour domestic producers (though this is now discouraged by the EEC), retraining schemes, and so on. The scale of the problem, and how it has changed over time, are illustrated in Table 3.1, showing regional unemployment rates.

Next, we come to *frictional unemployment*. This basically results when people seek to change jobs in a world of imperfect information. Such people might well register at a job centre, but only to facilitate search, and they soon find a job. The existence of reported vacancies is also an indication of imperfect information: firms cannot always locate the workers they need without some advertising or other form of search procedure. Thus in a normally functioning labour market, there will always be a stock of vacancies and some people temporarily and voluntarily unemployed while looking for jobs, even if the market is essentially in equilibrium.

One may, of course, wonder why people should choose to give up an existing job in order to find another: why should they not simply search for something else without giving up their original job? In the literature, two explanations are offered for this. First, it is argued (though in my view far from convincingly) that off-the-job search is more effective, since in a given time period more alternative jobs can be discovered and followed up. Secondly, the cost (in financial terms) of being unemployed for a short period may not be very high. The cost for a particular worker will depend on the prevailing income tax regime (for example, whether unemployment pay is taxable or not: until July 1982 it was not taxable in Britain, but now it is) and the family circumstances of the worker concerned, as well as on his or her income when working. Thus for workers with low enough short-term unemployment costs, off-the-job search may well be judged worthwhile.

The unemployment that corresponds to this situation is called frictional unemployment. Again, it calls for its own particular policy response; in this case the appropriate response is to take measures that can help the labour market to function more efficiently, such as opening more job centres, improving the flows of information about vacancies, facilitating moves to other areas, and perhaps even subsidizing job advertisements. In addition, measures to raise the short-term cost of being unemployed should reduce this kind of unemployment.

Finally, the unemployment that remains after the above three types have been accounted for is *demand deficient*, or as it is sometimes called, cyclical unemployment. It occurs, as the name suggests, when the level of aggregate demand in the economy (that is, the sum of consumption, government expenditure, investment and net exports) falls short of what would be required to hold overall unemployment down to just the first three categories (that is seasonal, structural and frictional). Thus in any given situation, economists tend to think of full employment as that level of economic activity which results in no demand deficient unemployment. This does not of course mean that the other forms of unemployment are just ignored, but rather that they require different types of policy response as indicated above: they will not be eliminated merely by an expansion of the economy.

Let us turn now from the unemployment rate itself to the incomes of the unemployed. It is sometimes suggested that the levels of social benefits – principally unemployment benefit and supplementary benefit – are so generous that many people prefer to remain unemployed and just live on the state. It is true that when someone with a good work record first becomes unemployed, his or her consumption (living standard) may not need to fall very much (for example, up to July 1982 because of tax rebates; thereafter, running down previous savings), but this situation is only temporary. Many of the poorest people in Britain are the unemployed with several young children to look after, and there is little evidence that many people actually choose to remain unemployed for long. Section 3.2 looks at the income of the unemployed and also comments on the cost to the exchequer of an increase in unemployment.

Section 3.3 then looks at some of the policy issues that arise in the context of unemployment, concentrating on measures to expand the level of demand. In discussing this, we also refer to the risks of stimulating faster wage and price inflation if expansion is too rapid.

3.2 INCOME OF THE UNEMPLOYED AND EXCHEQUER COSTS OF UNEMPLOYMENT

It is often suggested that nowadays, as compared to the thirties for instance, we need not feel so concerned about the unemployed because the state will assure them a reasonable income until they find work again. This myth is remarkably widely believed; it is important to realise, however, that many of the unemployed – especially the long-term unemployed and those with large families – are actually extremely poor. Some useful information about this question is presented in Burghes and Lister (1981). It seems that 'at the end of 1980, half of unemployed claiments were not receiving any unemployment benefit, more than a third of the unemployed (35 per cent) were totally dependent on supplementary benefit and just over 15 per cent were not receiving any benefit at all' (ibid., p. 83). Moreover, unemplovment benefits are set below the rates of means tested supplementary benefit (supposedly for incentive reasons), so that unemployed people with dependents often have to claim supplementary benefits as well. Table 3.2 (from ibid., p. 88) summarises the extent of poverty among the unemployed in two recent years:

Table 3.2   Numbers of people in families with unemployed head

	1974	*1977*
Below supplementary benefit level	90	290
Receiving supplementary benefit	360	980
Up to 40% above supplementary benefit level	90	200
Total	540	1470

Note: data in table are in thousands

In a more detailed study, Atkinson and Flemming (1978) investigated the replacement ratio, defined as the ratio between income plus benefits less taxes and housing outlays (allowing for rent and rate rebates) when unemployed relative to that when working. They found that the ratio depended quite sensitively on the following factors: gross earnings when in work, the duration of the unemployment spell, and the family type (number of dependents). For families with low incomes when in work and a large number of dependents, replacement ratios could exceed 100 per cent, that is, net resources available to the household could be greater when unemployed: but it should be remembered that such families represent a very small proportion of the population. For more typical households (single person, couple with one or two dependent children), replacement ratios were much lower unless their income when in work was less than half average earnings. Thus a high proportion of the unemployed (even when supplementary benefits are fully taken into account) have to contend with very substantial falls in real household income.

Returning to Burghes and Lister, their work also provides some interesting information on the costs of unemployment to the government. For 1980/81, when the average number of unemployed was just under two million, government outlays associated with unemployment were as follows:

	£m
Unemployment benefit	1176
Supplementary benefit	1235
Redundancy payments	242
Special employment measures	850
Rent and rate rebates	95
Administration	250
Total	3848

In addition, it has been estimated that each additional 100,000 unemployed will add about £135 million to government expenditure. Not only that, but the government also loses tax revenue when people are unemployed. For those registered as unemployed in 1980/81 (further amounts should be added for those not registered and for those on short time working), the revenue losses were as follows:

	£m
Income tax	1465
National insurance contributions	1540
Indirect taxes	265
Total	3270

Of course, some assumptions about the likely earnings of the unemployed had they been employed had to be made in order to obtain these estimates. However, I am sure the above figures at least give us the right order of magnitude. Indeed in a more recent study, Dilnot and Morris (1981) obtain a total cost of unemployment of £7807 million for 1980/81, though the coverage and method of estimation are not quite the same as for the figures reported above. They also estimate the corresponding figure for 1981/82 to be £12,947 million which, interestingly, is well above the public sector borrowing requirement (PSBR) for the same period. This figure is also given in the recent report from the House of Lords Select Committee on Unemployment (House of Lords, 1982, p. 53).

Overall, therefore, it is clear that unemployment is very expensive for the government, as well as for taxpayers, since tax rates are a good deal higher than they would otherwise need to be in order to finance unemployment at present high rates. This leads naturally on to a consideration of policies designed to reduce unemployment.

3.3 POLICIES TOWARDS UNEMPLOYMENT

These policies can take two principal forms. The first consists of a variety of ameliorative programmes, organized in Britain through the Manpower Services Commission to provide short-term employment, often with an element of training. Since the details of these programmes are discussed in Michael Jackson's chapter below, there is no need to dwell on them here. Suffice it to say that although such short-term measures serve to reduce the official unemployment figures, they can be disadvantageous in the longer term, for instance by preserving low-pay, low-productivity jobs in some areas or branches of the economy. Nevertheless, these programmes are clearly preferred by many of the unemployed to unemployment itself, and at least for some people they do provide the kind of training and experience that enables a more permanent job to be obtained.

The second kind of policy includes the whole range of macro-economic policy, directed towards a high employment objective. Beginning with the more conventional and established elements of policy, we have a range of fiscal and monetary measures to expand the economy. Since these measures are likely to affect both the balance of payments and the rate of inflation, they may well need to be supplemented by some policy towards the exchange rate (or, more radically, and more controversially by import controls), and by some form of anti-inflation policy, such as an incomes policy. At the very least, the fiscal and monetary policies designed to generate expansion in the economy are bound to be constrained by balance of payments or inflation considerations. The ways in which these various policies are likely to interact is, of course, a very complex matter. Partly because of this very real complexity, economists have sought to simplify the problem by focussing on a few key relationships. Unfortunately, different economists have developed different views about what the key relationships in the economy actually are, and this has given rise to a sometimes confusing range of policy implications. Moreover, the empirical study of macroeconomic relationships has not proved able to discriminate unambiguously between the alternative approaches to policy that have been put forward. Let us now examine some of the possibilities.

It has been well known since the publication of Keynes's *General Theory* that demand deficient unemployment could be reduced by expanding the economy using some combination of fisal and monetary policy. To generate expansion using fiscal policy, we either reduce tax rates, increase one or more components of government expenditure, or raise transfers such as pensions or social security payments. These changes in expenditures or taxes increase aggregate demand (by an amount that depends on the multiplier) and hence, unless the aggregate supply curve is vertical (see Prof. C. V. Brown's Chapter 2) equilibrium income is also raised. In order to produce the additional income, more people need to be employed, hence unemployment falls as required.

A similar effect can be generated somewhat less directly using monetary policy. In this case, a more relaxed monetary policy (that is, an expansion of the money supply) leads to a fall in interest rates and this in turn stimulates demand, especially private investment. From here the story is just as above and again unemployment falls. Thus if the above arguments are correct, standard Keynesian policies are indeed effective remedies for unemployment.

Much of what has now become the conventional core of macroeconomic theory is concerned with the detailed analysis of precisely these kinds of policy. Naturally, the specific effects in particular cases will depend on what taxes are to be changed, which components of government spending are to rise and how the monetary policy was put into effect. Thus a reduction in income tax will have somewhat different effects from a cut in employer's national insurance contributions, though both would be expansionary. Similarly, a decision to build more motorways will not have exactly the same effects as building more schools, or employing more staff in the health service to improve the quality of medical care; again, however, all these measures would be expansionary. In the post-war period, successive governments have used many variations on this theme in order to prevent unemployment from rising too far at times of recession. But their efforts were often constrained by balance of payments considerations, and more recently, governments have been so concerned about inflation in the economy that they have been willing to see unemployment rise to levels that would have been quite inconceivable a decade ago.

The connection between the level of employment and the balance of payments is quite easy to understand. It is simply this: as the economy expands, it is likely that more imports will be sucked into the country as part of the additional demand is met from overseas, but there is little reason to expect a corresponding rise in demand for our exports since that depends on the state of demand in foreign markets. Consequently, the balance of trade is very likely to deteriorate, unless our own expansion coincides with expansion in the countries forming our principal overseas markets. Now that we operate with a system of flexible exchange rates (in contrast to the fixed exchange rates that prevailed before 1971) and benefit from North Sea Oil, the balance of payments constraint on economic activity has become much less severe than it used to be: Chapter 6 provides a fuller discussion of this point. On the other hand, Britain's competitive position in world markets has deteriorated alarmingly in recent years, with our exports losing ground and many industries suffering from rapidly increasing import penetration. This observation has led some economists to argue that the conventional expansionary policies discussed above should be supplemented by import controls to ensure that the additional domestic demand does not merely lead to higher imports. However, protecting domestic industry in this way is a risky policy for a number of reasons. Briefly, it invites retaliation from other countries, which would adversely affect our exports; it provides an opportunity, but not necessarily much incentive, for import-competing industries to take steps to improve their productivity and become competitive again; and it is likely to involve a complex bureaucracy to administer the controls which in turn provides new opportunities for lobbying and manipulation.

Turning to inflation, at least since the late 1950s it has been appreciated that low levels of unemployment were associated with relatively rapid rates of wage (and hence price) inflation. The well-known Phillips curve expresses this relationship most clearly. The association makes sense in a relatively free labour market since as employment increases (and so unemployment falls) workers' bargaining position in relation to employers strengthens, so wage offers are likely to become more generous. The converse holds when employment is relatively low or falling rapidly. This inverse relationship between money wage increases and the rate of unemployment will also depend on the current rate of price inflation (since this affects workers' views about the likely development of real wages), and may also be influenced by various government policies that could affect expectations.

The latter includes incomes policy, and other less formal means of intervention into the normal wage bargaining process, though the incomes policies that we have experienced in the past have only been successful for fairly short periods. Recently there have been some suggestions about a tax-based incomes policy, whereby the amount of tax firms pay would depend on the wage awards they granted. Thus the aim would be to operate an incomes policy by means of economic incentives, rather than by coercion; however, this idea has not yet been tried out, so it is hard to judge how successful it would be in practice. The present Conservative government has not sought to operate a formal incomes policy, although it inevitably exerts great influence over public-sector pay, as do all governments. The next chapter examines incomes policy in more detail.

Already under the last Labour government, and much more so since 1979, British governments have abandoned their traditional faith in Keynesian remedies for unemployment. We have already outlined the kinds of fiscal and monetary policy needed to generate economic expansion, and hence reduce unemployment, according to Keynesian views of the economy's functioning. But by the mid-1970s it appeared that this kind of remedy only offered a short-term palliative. Although it generated some expansion initially, in the longer run either the expansion would peter out or be reversed, or inflation would accelerate.

For *Keynesians* the problem here involves the important interactions between fiscal and monetary policy, frequently neglected in introductory accounts of macroeconomic theory. For instance, if expansion is brought about by an increase in government expenditure, it is clear, even allowing for the extra tax revenue generated by the higher level of income, that the Public Sector Borrowing Requirement (PSBR) will increase. This increase must be financed, either by the Bank of England selling more government bonds to the public, or by issuing more money or a combination of the two. In the case of bonds, in order to persuade the private sector to buy and hold more of them, interest rates would have to go up. But this would discourage private investment, so at least part of the government-led expansion would be offset by private sector contraction. This is the simplest form of what is known as *crowding out*. If the increased PSBR is financed instead by monetary expansion, then interest rates might even fall, so that initially at least, private and public sector activity would be mutually reinforcing. However, according to monetarist theories of inflation, substantial reliance on monetary expansion soon generates inflationary pressures. The resulting inflation both increases uncertainty in the economy, which tends to discourage investment, and calls forth a deflationary policy response from the government. On this view, it is easy to see how stop-go cycles of the kind that characterized British economic policy up to the mid-1970s might have arisen.

Equally, one can understand (even if one doesn't agree with the new approach) the government's present determination to concentrate on eliminating inflation and its rejection of Keynesian remedies. The new *monetarist* approach has led to much higher unemployment than expected when the policy was first adopted but if the theories behind the new approach are correct, much of the unemployment should be temporary and the economy should eventually start to grow again along a healthier path. However, it remains to be seen whether the recent move away from conventional demand management (which is considered successful in the short run, but with undesirable longer term effects like inflation and generally poor economic performance) towards monetarist policies (which bring short-term difficulties like high unemployment, but which, according to the relevant theory, should perform better in the longer term) will succeed in improving Britain's economic outlook for the 1980s. Many observers and commentators are not at present very hopeful, but it is too soon to be sure.

REFERENCES

Atkinson, A. B. and Flemming, J. S. (1978) 'Unemployment, Social Security and Incentives', *Midland Bank Review*, Autumn, pp. 6–16.

Barker, T. (1982) 'Long Term Recovery: A Return To Full Employment', *Lloyds Bank Review*, January, pp. 19–35.

Burghes, L. and Lister, R. (1981) *Unemployment: Who Pays the Price?* Poverty Pamphlet 53 (London: Child Poverty Action Group), November.

Dilnot, A. W. and Morris, C. N. (1981) 'The Exchequer Costs of Unemployment', *Fiscal Studies*, Vol. 2 (3), November, pp. 10–19.

Hawkins, K. (1979) *Unemployment* (Harmondsworth: Penguin Books).

House of Lords (1982) *Report from the Select Committee of the House of Lords on Unemployment*, HL 142 (1981/82) (London: HMSO).

Keynes, J. M. (1936) *The General Theory of Employment, Interest and Money* (London: Macmillan).

Shackleton, J. R. (1982) 'Economists and Unemployment', *National Westminster Bank Quarterly Review*, February, pp. 13–30.

Tomlinson, J. (1983) 'Does Mass Unemployment Matter?' *National Westminster Bank Quarterly Review*, February, pp. 35–45.

Sinfield, A. (1981) *What Unemployment Means,* (Oxford; Martin Robertson).

QUESTIONS FOR DISCUSSION

1   What are the main types of unemployment?
2   Which groups in the population are most affected by unemployment?
3   Why is the government reluctant to expand the economy quickly to bring down unemployment?
4   What are the costs of unemployment?
5   Critically examine the view that unemployment is currently so high in Britain because wage rates are too high.
6   What is the likely impact of technological change on unemployment? (Note: take care to consider both the supply and demand for labour; see also Chapter 8.)
7   What is frictional unemployment? How can government policy help to reduce it?
8   How would you expect unemployment to be affected by cuts in unemployment benefit and other social security payments to

those seeking work?
9 What effect do job creation and related government-supported schemes have on the rate of unemployment? (See also Chapter 9.).

4 The Political Economy of Inflation

PETER BIRD

4.1 INTRODUCTION

The present British government has stated publicly on a number of occasions that it regards the control of inflation as its overriding priority. This fact alone is sufficient testimony to the importance of inflation in current economic policy discussion. In this chapter, we consider four important questions concerning inflation and public policy.

What do we mean by inflation and how is it measured? Why is inflation a problem? What are its causes? How can it be cured? Restrictions on length mean that many issues cannot be explored as much as is desirable. However, at the end of the chapter there are a number of suggestions for further reading on the topics discussed.

4.2 THE MEASUREMENT OF INFLATION

Inflation is a rise in the aggregate price level; that is, a rise in the price of goods and services in general. When the price of an individual commodity rises we must distinguish between the relative and absolute components of the increase. As an example, consider the price of my bus fare to work which has risen from 50p this time last year (1982) to 56p today. However, over the same period the aggregate price level has increased by four per cent. Thus, of the 12 per cent nominal price increase in the bus fare, 4 per cent can be attributed to inflation, and 8 per cent is the increase in the real or relative price of the bus. Changes in relative prices do not constitute inflation, although they are invariably a feature of inflationary periods.

To measure inflation we need to consider the prices of all goods and services. In practice this is done by comparing the price of a 'basket' of commodities purchased by the average consumer. The most common measure is the retail price index (RPI) which is based on a basket of 600 goods and services, and is published monthly by the Department of Employment. The proportion in which commodities enter the RPI basket is an approximation to the spending habits of the average consumer, as determined by expenditure surveys. However, the number of goods in the basket is deliberately restricted in order that the RPI can be computed quickly and regularly.

There are three major problems with using the RPI to measure inflation. The first is that there is no such person as the 'average' consumer. Each person consumes a different basket of goods and is personally affected by inflation in a different way. This can be particularly important for old-age pensioners who spend considerably larger proportions of their incomes on food and energy than do younger people. For this reason the Department of Employment also publishes a separate price index based upon pensioners' needs; in fact, this index has moved in a very similar way to the RPI in recent years.

The second problem is that the basket of purchases of the average consumer changes over time, in response to shifting tastes, changes in relative prices, and the availability of new products. For example, a much greater proportion of the average food budget is now spent on processed chicken, and a much smaller proportion on wet fish, than in previous years. The index has to be reweighted in order to take account of such changes. Since reweighting of the RPI is undertaken only periodically, there are times when it overestimates the impact of inflation by ignoring shifts in expenditure towards cheaper goods. Nevertheless it is generally accepted that the RPI is a reasonably accurate indicator of changes in the overall price level.

The third problem arises when the RPI is used in conjunction with indices of earnings to derive indicators of living standards. This problem became acute in 1979 when the incoming Conservative government engineered a shift in the taxation burden from direct (income) tax towards indirect (value-added) taxation. Although designed to be neutral in its effect on overall living standards, the shift was reflected in an increase of about 4 per cent in the RPI. Consequently the government has also published, since 1979, a tax and price index (TPI) which takes account of both inflation and changes in the tax burden, direct and indirect. However, in public discussion of inflation, the RPI is still the indicator commonly used.

The rate of inflation is the change in the price level during some agreed time period. The choice of this period has on occasions led to confusion and controversy. The generally accepted procedure now is to measure inflation over the immediately preceding twelve-month period. Thus, at the time of writing, the most recently published inflation rate is 3.7 per cent for the increase in the RPI between the middle of May 1982 and the middle of May 1983, expressed as a percentage of the May 1982 level of the RPI. The procedure means that current trends for inflation to accelerate or decelerate are given only the same weight as the trends of eleven months ago. However, the measure has the advantage of being objective and unambiguous, and cannot be misrepresented by unscrupulous politicians.

Table 4.1   British inflation 1963–82

Percentage increases in RPI over previous year			
1963	2.0	1973	9.2
1964	3.2	1974	16.1
1965	4.8	1975	24.2
1966	3.9	1976	16.5
1967	2.4	1977	15.8
1968	4.8	1978	8.3
1969	5.4	1979	13.4
1970	6.3	1980	18.0
1971	9.4	1981	11.9
1972	7.1	1982	8.6
		1983*	3.7

* May figure

SOURCE: *Economic Trends*

Table 4.1 and Figure 4.1 show the annual average rate of inflation measured on the above basis between 1962 and 1983. It shows how the inflation rate edged up very slowly throughout the 1960s. In the early 1970s it spurted upwards to a peak of 9 per cent. It then fell back slighly and soared in 1975 to a record post-war rate of over 24 per cent. From then it declined steadily, before rising again in 1979 and 1980 to a level of 18 per cent. The rate fell again in 1981, and has fallen rapidly through 1982 and 1983. Most commentators expect that it will rise again modestly over the next year. It is easy to see why historians will probably refer to the last decade as the Inflationary Seventies.

Figure 4.1　　British inflation, 1963–82

4.3 THE COSTS OF INFLATION

It appears to be unchallenged in public policy debates that inflation is a 'bad thing'. Indeed, as emphasized at the beginning of Chapter 2, the present government has made the reduction of inflation virtually the sole target of its economic policy. It is instructive, however, to consider exactly what are the true costs of inflation. In doing so it is helpful to distinguish between inflation which is *anticipated*, and taken into account in economic transactions, and inflation which is *unanticipated*, and not expected. It is also helpful to correct some common misconceptions about the effects of inflation.

　　Most inflations to date have been unanticipated, to the extent that they have not been completely allowed for in all transactions. The most important consequences have been distributional. Since most contracts in our economy are still denominated in money terms, those persons owing money (debtors) have gained, and those lending money (creditors) have lost from inflation. Suppose you lend me money for a year at an interest rate of 7 per cent, expecting prices to rise by 5 per cent during the year. Your expected real return on this loan is 2 per cent. Suppose, however, that your anticipation of inflation is imperfect, and that prices actually rise by 10 per cent. Your real return will be negative at −3 per cent. The creditor (you) loses; the debtor (me) gains.

Two examples of redistribution in the inflationary seventies were in the housing market, and the market for government securities (the national debt). Owner-occupiers, who borrowed from building societies to finance house purchase gained at the expense of building society investors; and governments (and ultimately future taxpayers) gained as inflation reduced the value of the national debt; the losers were those who put their trust in government securities.

As the distributional effects of inflation have been experienced, more effort has been devoted to anticipating inflation, or to correcting its effects. The most important response has been indexation. The government now makes available to the public bonds whose value is linked to the RPI. Once known popularly as 'granny bonds', these provide a vehicle by which savers can preserve the real value of their assets. Similarly, social security and other government benefits are now annually uprated in line with the RPI, to preserve the real incomes of beneficiaries. Tax thresholds are revised in the same way, to avoid the real tax burden being affected by inflation. In 1981 the government declined to undertake such revision in its entirety. In these circumstances, the distributional effect was an explicit policy choice, and not an unanticipated effect of inflation.

What then are the costs of an inflation which is completely anticipated, or compensated in indexation contracts? Two such sets of costs are commonly cited, and both are relatively minor. The first are known as 'shoe-leather costs'. The one contract which cannot be indexed is that of holding the means of payment, that is, cash in the pocket or bank current accounts. When the inflation rate rises so does the opportunity cost of holding non-indexed money, and the demand for money balances consequently falls. In practice, this means that individuals economize by holding less money in their wallets, purses, or current accounts, and making more trips to the bank or building society to withdraw deposits. This explains the term 'shoe-leather' costs. We could note in passing that the 'trouser-pocket' benefits of carrying fewer coins are assumed to be of less importance!

The second set of costs have been called 'menu costs'. These are incurred simply because inflation causes real resources to be devoted to marking up prices. Reprinting restaurant menus, adjusting pay telephones, and changing note and coin denominations are typical examples of these costs. It is hard to avoid the conclusion that costs of this type are fairly trivial. The shoe-leather and menu costs of fully anticipated inflation do not represent a major burden on society.

More serious are costs of the third type. These arise from the fact that inflation can be anticipated, and that resources are devoted to the process of anticipation. Not only are these resources (primarily managerial time) diverted from alternative productive uses, but the structure of incentives in the economy is also affected. In inflationary times, businesses thrive or prosper not as they provide good or bad products and services, but as their managers correctly or incorrectly anticipate inflation. Inflation rewards speculative rather than entre-preneurial abilities. It is far from fanciful to assert that this factor has been an important contributor to Britain's current economic malady.

Although we have seen that both anticipated and unanticipated inflation have substantial costs, in popular discussion the costs are often exaggerated. A common belief is that inflation harms Britain's trade performance by making exports uncompetitive. This is false in the way it is popularly believed. Inflation can harm export competi-tiveness only if the exchange rate does not freely adjust to maintain foreign exchange equilibrium. If it fails to do so because of Central Bank intervention or speculative capital movements, then it is these factors and not the inflation which are to blame.

Another common misconception is that of the worker who claims to be worse off because of inflation. However, wages in a pure inflation increase by the same amount as prices. If one section of the work force does not obtain a wage increase which compensates for price rises, then the fall in real income should be seen as a change in the real wage structure, not as an effect of inflation. Remember, however, that the real resource costs identified above must be borne somewhere in the economy. Suppose that company A performs badly over a long period because of excess managerial time being devoted to anticipating inflation, and too little time to product development. Suppose that the company consequently pays wages lower than those paid in previously comparable industries. In these circumstances, the employees of company A *can* genuinely claim to be worse off on account of inflation.

Although we have identified some of the real costs of inflation, it is not obvious how these could ever be quantified. However, it is important to put them into some perspective. It is difficult to envisage how their magnitude could ever approach that of the current unemployment problem. Compared to both the real output loss implied by an unemployment rate above three million, and the human misery of being jobless, the costs of inflation in Britain today are surely of a much lower order.

4.4 THE NATURE OF THE INFLATIONARY PROCESS

Inflation is a dynamic process. We therefore need to explain not only why inflation starts, but also how it continues, and the circumstances in which it accelerates or decelerates. It is the whole process, rather than simply the origin of inflation, that is consequently the subject of this section.

In the market for a single commodity, an upward shift in either the supply or the demand curve will cause an increase in price. Consider a competitive market such as that for tomatoes. A reduction in supply caused, for example, by bad weather, or an increase in demand caused by a change in consumer tastes, will both lead to an increase in price. It is not possible to explain inflation in the whole economy in this simple way. Inflation is a dynamic process of increasing prices, not a one-off upward shift. Also, there are three important differences between the single market for tomatoes and the complex system of markets that constitutes our economy.

First, competitive markets are rare in our economy. In many industries wage levels are set by negotiations with monopolistic trade unions. Other industries often follow the outcome of such bargains. Product prices are set by firms with varying degrees of market power. This means that prices and wages can be moved independently of demand and supply effects. Firms in oligopolistic industries can raise prices simply to increase profit margins, perhaps in order to finance a new investment programme. Workers in powerful trade unions can enforce wage increases irrespective of whether there has been an increase in the demand for labour. This ability of firms and workers to move prices independently is sometimes described as a 'cost-push', as opposed to a 'demand-pull', influence on the price level.

The second difference is that at the level of the national economy, demand and supply are closely linked. For the economy as a whole, total supply must equal total demand. The money paid in wages to workers is an aggregate cost, but it is also an important component of demand for the economy's output. This means that shifts in the cost function and shifts in aggregate demand cannot be treated in isolation: they work together in sustaining the inflationary process. Suppose, for example, that there is an initial cost-push stimulus caused by higher wages being negotiated across the economy. This will produce an upward shift of the supply curve in the goods market. At the same time, however, the larger wage packets mean increased aggregate demand, and thus an upward shift of the demand curve (a 'demand-pull' effect) in the goods market. This example shows how once inflation is in progress it is impossible to separate demand-pull and cost-push influences. The concept remains helpful only for identifying the initial cause of the inflation.

The third difference is one of degree. Two very important influences on the economy as a whole are the government, disbursing expenditure and collecting taxes, and the foreign sector through international trade. In some circumstances a single market can also be affected very significantly by government actions and foreign trade. Many markets, however, can be analysed with little regard to these influences. For the whole economy the government and foreign sectors are crucial in the analysis of inflation. Government expenditure very often represents the demand-pull impetus which causes inflation to accelerate. Increases in the prices of imported raw materials have in the past been an important cost-push contribution from the foreign sector. They were particularly important in the acceleration of inflation in 1973; more recently, falls in world commodity prices have been a major reason for the rapid fall in inflation in 1982 and 1983.

A helpful way to understand the inflationary process is as a conflict over the distribution of national output. This output has to be divided between a number of competing claims. Employees claim it for personal consumption from wages; company managers have claims for investment from retained profits; shareholders claim their personal consumption from dividends. Central and local governments register claims for social expenditure from rates and taxes. Through foreign trade, the overseas sector also makes a claim on national output. This is a crude categorization; the model can be made more detailed if necessary. For the distribution to be feasible, the sum of separate claims must not exceed the total of the economy's output.

In a free economy there is no prior mechanism to ensure that the claims on output are mutually compatible. If claims do exceed the total output of the economy, the distribution is not feasible. This situation can be resolved in only two ways. Either one or more parties can be forced effectively to reduce their claims on output. This occurs when an anti-inflationary policy is successful. Alternatively, the claims can all be satisfied, but not at the same point in time. Inflation is the mechanism through which this occurs.

Consider again the example of inflation arising from an initial cost-push impetus in the labour market. In the first time period, workers successfully negotiate a large pay award. Their claim on output is satisfied in this period; their employers' claim on output is not. In the next time period, prices are raised. Profit margins are restored, and it is the employers' claim on output which is satisfied. The real value of the wage claim is lost; in this time-period the workers' claim on output is frustrated. In the next time period, the workers will respond with a fresh pay claim; and so the process continues. A similar story can be told for inflationary experiences arising from alternative initial stimuli.

The above model of the inflationary process has a number of advantages. First, it emphasizes the social and political nature of inflation, as a conflict over distributional shares. It cannot be seen solely as a technical economic problem, divorced from its political context. Secondly, it provides a general framework which incorporates cost-push and demand-pull influences. It is an interesting exercise for the reader to explain particular historical examples of inflation in terms of the model. The third advantage of seeing inflation in this way is that it provides an excellent framework for analysing counter-inflation policies.

4.5 POLICIES AGAINST INFLATION

The essence of any policy to eliminate inflation is the reduction of demands of at least one group in the economy so that the overall claims on output are mutually compatible. Governments can achieve this in two general ways. One is to affect the various claims on output through implementing monetary and fiscal policies. The other is to influence claims directly by using the government's legislative and executive powers in the implementation of prices and incomes policies.

The present government is pursuing methods of the first kind. Their main emphasis is on monetary policy. Money acts as a lubricant in the inflationary process. Consider a process in which wages and prices are chasing each other upwards at a rate of 10 per cent per year. In normal circumstances the money needed by economic transactors to finance normal business would also need to increase at the same rate. In years up to 1975 British governments more or less ensured this by increasing the supply of money at a similar rate. The policy was known as 'accommodating' the inflation. More recently, however, governments have attempted to restrain the inflation by refusing to accommodate the increase. The immediate effect of such restriction is to squeeze company cash flows. From this we can envisage a number of different scenarios in which the inflationary process is suppressed.

In scenario I the squeeze on company cash flows leads directly to some company bankruptcies. Other companies compete against each other for funds bidding up the interest rate in doing so. The higher interest rate, by increasing loan repayments can itself force more companies into bankruptcy. In addition, the higher interest rate will reduce company investment and consumer spending, leading to lower aggregate demand. The result is further bankruptcies and lay-offs of employees. How is the sequence to end? It does so when employers stop passing on wage increases as higher prices. Instead firms compete against each other to lower profit margins and increase market share. This lessens upward pressure on wages, and the inflationary process subsides and the pressure on cash flows is abated. In this scenario the policy of monetary restriction works by reducing the claim of profits on national output.

In scenario II the initial unfolding of events is similar. The only difference is in how the policy has its ultimate effect. In this second scenario workers in the labour market respond directly to bankruptcies by reducing the pressure on wages. This is because unemployment removes bargaining power by offering the unemployed as competitors to the employed. Even more so, the threat of unemployment reduces worker militancy. The effect is to halt the inflationary process from within the labour market. The benefits of lower costs then feed into the product market. Thus in this scenario the policy of monetary restriction acts to reduce the claim of wages on output.

With both scenarios monetary restriction causes deflation of output until inflation is squeezed out of the system. Recent work in theoretical economics has stressed the additional role that expectations can play. If agents in the product market and the labour market correctly foresee the anti-inflationary impact of monetary restriction, then they will modify their claims without the necessity for deflation actually to occur. In these circumstances monetary restriction squeezes inflation out of the system painlessly. In this scenario III, monetary restriction, aided by what are known as 'rational' expectations, reduces inflation immediately in the demand and cost sides of the market.

Clearly monetary restriction is a more attractive proposition with Scenario III. Unfortunately, despite its theoretical nicety, there is no reason to suppose that the scenario makes practical sense in the Britain of today. For the theory to work, it requires that the mass of the population, workers and employers, consumers and sellers, accepts its validity. Since even most professional economists are sceptical, this appears to be an over-ambitious requirement. The failure of the theory is indicated by actual experience. One adjective that cannot be applied to the effects of monetary restriction in Britain since 1976 is 'painless'.

With scenarios I and II monetary restriction works through the deflation of output. However, a similar deflation can be obtained without monetary restriction. This can be achieved by means of fiscal policy – specifically by the reduction of government expenditure or the increase of taxation. By reducing aggregate demand and increasing unemployment, fiscal restriction can be used to reduce inflation.

Similar scenarios to those above can be envisaged, influencing either workers or employers in the same way.

In our discussion so far, we have for convenience of exposition simplified the problem while attempting to describe its main features. At this stage, however, we must enter two qualifications to our analysis. The first is that the various scenarios discussed are not necessarily independent of one another. Deflationary policies typically work on both wages and profits, and they can be aided if only partially by agents' expectations. In addition, fiscal and monetary restriction are typically pursued in tandem, rather than as alternative policies. One of the many ways to reduce the growth of the money supply is by reducing the Public Sector Borrowing Requirement (PSBR); this usually implies also a fiscal deflation of aggregate demand. The deflation in Britain since 1979 has been as much the result of fiscal as of monetary restriction, as is admitted by official sources. It is interesting that although both the British and the United States administrations would broadly claim to be 'monetarist', the course pursued by the Reagan administration in the US has not involved fiscal restriction; indeed an expansionary fiscal policy has been pursued alongside the policy of monetary restriction.

The second qualification is that the international sector of the economy represents another route by which monetary restriction deflates the economy (this is covered more fully in Chapter 6). High interest rates encourage speculative capital flows, and these can maintain the foreign exchange value of the currency above its equilibrium level. This reduces the sales of exports, with a deflationary effect upon demand. Deflation of output via this route has been an important feature of recent British experience.

There is an inherent weakness in using monetary and fiscal policies to reduce inflation, in that they work by sacrificing some of the economy's output. In itself, this makes the original incompatible claims on output even more excessive with respect to the new lower output. Consequently, the reduction of claims has to be greater than it otherwise would have been. This means that the costs of reducing inflation by monetary and fiscal measures can be very high. The present government's policy has been very expensive in terms of lost output.

Prices and incomes policies do not have this defect. They operate by reducing claims on the national product by direct government action. No sacrifice of output is required. For this reason prices and incomes policies have for a long time been proposed as an alternative to traditional monetary and fiscal anti-inflationary policies.

Prices and incomes policies (often referred to simply as incomes policies) have been pursued in various ways and at various times over the last fifteen years in most of the world's developed economies. They have been voluntary or compulsory; have operated on wages and on salaries only, or also on prices; and have been applied rigidly, or flexibly with exceptions. There is no doubt that at least in the short term such policies successfully reduce inflation, and they do so without the sacrifice of output or the misery of unemployment. However, they have encountered a number of problems at both the political and the economic level.

The political objections to prices and incomes policies have come from both the left and right. The grounds have been that they interfere with freedom, either of collective bargaining, or of price setting. Also trade unionists and company executives have resented what they interpret as being 'blamed' for inflation. During the pursuit of income policies political opposition has grown, and opponents have capitalized on the economic problems associated with the policies. As a result, governments in democratic societies have been forced to abandon or to modify severely their incomes policies before attainment of the declared policy goals. The previous three UK governments were voted from office after the collapse of unpopular incomes policies. Significantly, perhaps, the current government recently triumphed at the election after a period in office in which it had firmly eschewed incomes policies of any kind.

The major economic problem associated with incomes policies is that they suppress the normal operation of the market. In a market economy the continuous changes in products, technology, and tastes require that relative prices should be able to change freely. Although this is consistent with a stable aggregate price level, it requires that any incomes policy rules be capable of distinguishing between relative and absolute price changes. No incomes policy has yet been successful in this area. The result has been relative price distortions, and consequent losses in allocative efficiency. Particularly with respect to labour market differentials, the distortions have also led to political discord.

A common criticism of incomes policies is that they can succeed only in the short-run, and that inflationary pressure reappears when the policy restrictions are removed. There is reasonable statistical support for this objection. This criticism applies validly to those policies which have been pursued in the past and have ultimately failed at the political level. However, the supporters of incomes policies claim to have learned the lessons, and are now searching for policies that can be operated over medium and long periods. Recent examples are proposals by the Labour party for a 'national economic assessment', and by members of the Alliance parties for an incomes policy enforced through the tax system.

The same criticism can be made of the policy on demand deflation. Firms cannot prosper indefinitely on depressed profit margins. Nor can using unemployment to squash workers' aspirations prevent them seeking to regain lost ground when bargaining prospects improve. It is possible to find good statistical support also for this objection. The response to it has come from leading members of the Conservative party. They diagnose the problem as the structure of our economy, with its monopolistic trade unions and oligopolistic companies. If these distortions are removed, and the government controls strictly its own claims on national output, then incompatible demands on total output cannot be enforced. If politicians are prepared to adopt this political path, then it should be possible to control inflation without any unacceptable sacrifices of the economy's output.

4.6 CONCLUSIONS

The main conclusion of the previous sections is that although inflation manifests itself as an economic phenomenon, its underlying causes lie within the political and social framework. It follows that the problem of inflation cannot be resolved by some technical or economic 'fix'. Policy to reduce inflation involves hard political choices in which the costs of counter-inflation policy must be counted against the costs of the inflation itself. To avoid inflation completely it is necessary for society to find a mechanism for distributing its output among competing claims without economic conflict. The present British government regards the unemployment costs of its current policy as justified by the benefits of reducing inflation. Many of its members believe that by reforming our institutions the recurrence of inflation can be avoided in the future. Opponents of the government, possessing a different set of value judgements, would dissent from both propositions.

SUGGESTIONS FOR FURTHER READING

Andrews, P. and Evans, G. (1980) *Inflation and the Phillips Curve*, Stirling Economics Teaching Paper 3.

Bootle, R. (1981) 'How Important is it to Defeat Inflation: The Evidence', *Three Banks Review*, December.

Burton, J. (1982) 'The Varieties of Monetarism and their Policy Implications', *Three Banks Review*, June.

Cobham, D. (1978) 'The Politics of the Economics of Inflation', *Lloyds Bank Review*, April.

Dow, A. C. (1980) *Monetarism and Inflation* Stirling Economics Teaching Paper 1.

Flemming, J. S. (1976) *Inflation* (Oxford: Oxford University Press).

Higham, D. and Tomlinson, J. (1982) 'Why do Governments Worry about Inflation?', *National Westminister Bank Quarterly Review,* May.

Jones, A. *(1973) The New Inflation* (Harmondsworth: Penguin Books).

Kaldor, Lord N. (1982) *The Scourge of Monetarism* (Oxford: Oxford University Press).

Kaldor, Lord N. (1983) 'The Role of Commodity Prices in Economic Recovery', *Lloyds Bank Review,* July.

Rowley, C. and Wiseman, J. (1983) 'Inflation versus Unemployment: Is the Government Impotent?', *National Westminster Bank Quarterly Review,* February.

Trevithick, J. (1977) *Inflation* (Harmondsworth: Penguin Books).

QUESTIONS FOR DISCUSSION

1   Discuss the problem of constructing an index to compare the levels of consumer prices in the UK and in Italy.
2   Are there any benefits from inflation?
3   Can inflation occur in centrally planned economies such as the USSR?
4   Why does inflation typically accelerate in a country at war?
5   Do trade unions cause inflation?
6   What form would you propose for an incomes policy for Britain in 1984?

5 Monetary Policy in a Speculative Environment

PETER E. EARL AND SHEILA C. DOW

5.1 INTRODUCTION

A successful active monetary policy depends on monetary variables having a powerful and consistent influence on other economic variables. There is however a view that financial markets (as well as goods markets) are subject to unstable shifts in both demand and supply as a result of shifts in expectations. The formation of expectations and acting upon them we call here 'speculation'. Speculation is not limited to wealthy participants in the stock market – it extends to consumption and production decisions, as well as to more general choices between financial assets. It is the purpose of this chapter to outline this alternative view of the speculative environment in which monetary policy operates, in comparison with the more conventional, non-speculative view.

John Maynard Keynes, the father of modern macroeconomics, was not only an academic economist; he also made a fortune by speculating on the London stock market. His theoretical writing, in particular his (1936) *General Theory of Employment, Interest and Money*, seems to have been influenced considerably by his experience as a speculator. However, while economists since Keynes made considerable use of concepts he developed, such as the consumption function, most have played down the role he assigned to speculation. Speculation is given a part to play only as one motive for demanding money. Not only does this suggest that speculation plays no other part in the economy, but even that part has been diminished in importance as alternative reasons were put forward for the demand for money to be a function of the rate of interest.

The neglect of the speculative dimension of economic activity has had a significant impact on policy matters, particularly in the conduct of monetary policy under the Conservative government since 1979.

In this chapter we attempt to show how analysis of the economy is developed once speculation is incorporated as a central feature, with particular reference to monetary policy. It is shown that, rather than advocating control of interest rates or monetary growth at particular target rates, the speculative perspective suggests that monetary policy should be geared to promoting the stability of interest rates, and allowing the money supply to grow in line with demand. The chapter draws on the work of two economists who have *not* neglected Keynes' work on speculation, George Shackle (1974) and Hyman Minsky (1976).

In the next section, a brief outline is given of the conventional theory of monetary policy where speculation plays no significant role. The third section outlines the way in which speculation affects expenditure in general, while the fourth concentrates on speculation in financial markets, and the fifth on speculation and financial institutions. The concluding section includes a policy package, suggested by the theory developed in the previous sections.

5.2 MONETARY POLICY IN A NON-SPECULATIVE ENVIRONMENT

Speculation features in the conventional theory of monetary policy, if at all, as one of the motives for holding money, as suggested by Keynes himself. If money is held as an asset, rather than solely to finance specific expenditures, then the future value of *alternative* assets is of considerable importance. If other assets are likely to appreciate in value, then it makes no sense to hold money instead; on the other hand, money is preferable to a depreciating asset. When new assets are issued with lower interest rates than existing assets, the latter become more attractive and their prices rise; the reverse is true if new assets are issued with increased interest rates. So the speculative demand for money is low (and the demand for alternative assets is high) if interest rates are expected to fall and is high if interest rates are likely to rise. On the simplistic assumption that high interest rates are likely to fall and low interest rates are likely to rise, we can say that the speculative demand for money is a negative function of the current rate of interest. This statement encapsulates the *neo-classical synthesis* version of Keynes's theory of speculative demand.

But many economists were uncomfortable with the notion that money was held as an asset, a store of wealth; since money earns no interest, surely other assets would always be preferable. Empirical studies, however, did seem to show that actual money holdings did follow some pattern along with the rate of interest. Rather than accepting the Keynesian notion of the speculative demand for money, however, the reaction was to find other reasons for the rate of interest to influence the demand for money. One of the two major alternatives was put forward by Baumol (1952), arguing that the interest rate was the opportunity cost of holding money. If the rate of interest rose, then the *transactions* demand for money fell because the opportunity cost of holding money had risen. The other major explanation, put forward by Tobin (1958), attempted to preserve the speculative demand concept by arguing that interest rates acted partly as compensation for the risk of changes in assets' value. People thus spread risk by holding a variety of assets, ranging from money with no interest but no risk to assets with high interest rates but high risk.

The upshot of these developments was that there appeared to be a stable relationship between the rate of interest and the demand for money. Meanwhile, monetarists were developing the argument that there was a stable relationship between the amount of money in the economy and total expenditure, and thus the price level. Keynesians were emphasizing rather the relationship between the rate of interest and investment, which in turn determined total expenditure via the multiplier. Whichever way you looked at it, there seemed to be a stable relationship between both money holdings and the rate of interest, and total expenditure.

Further, the process by which the money supply was generated was also viewed as being stable. Traditionally, the process was described by the money multiplier, which demonstrated how new reserves introduced into the banking system could support a much larger amount of loans and deposits, since banks are only required to hold a proportion of deposits as reserves. But the degree to which banks could increase loans and attract deposits depended on the interest rate, and the multiplier itself was shown to be a function of the interest rate. Further, new reserves entered the banking system primarily in response to demand, which in turn was a function of the rate of interest. As long as the central bank undertakes to meet any demand, through the Lender of Last Resort facility, the supply of money is determined by demand; both can only be controlled by controlling the rate of interest, raising it to choke off demand. This the Bank of England can do by adding to market demand or supply, as appropriate, to influence the market price. The Bank can choose to set a money supply target by manipulating the interest rate or vice versa.

From the mid 1970s, the main aim of macroeconomic policy was the control of inflation, by the control of aggregate expenditure. Monetary policy seemed to be appropriate, since controlling either the rate of interest or the money supply would control total expenditure, according to both Keynesians and monetarists. The main debate among policy theorists thus centres on whether the Bank of England should concentrate on the rate of interest or on the money supply. Either would do as long as the demand for money was a stable function of the interest rate. A rise in interest rates would reduce the demand for money; alternatively a fall in the supply of money relative to demand would cause interest rates to rise. Keynesians argued for interest rate control, because it had a more direct effect on expenditure by discouraging investment. Monetarists argued for money supply control because it would have the more direct effect on both consumer and investment expenditure (although helped along by higher interest rates). There were further debates about whether it was a practical proposition to control the money supply in the first place. While the government's (1980) Green Paper on Monetary Control advocated a move towards direct control of the money supply by controlling bank reserves (the 'monetary base'), the greater emphasis in practice has remained on interest rates. Policy is expressed now in terms of target ranges for these money supply definitions, but without rigid adherence to the targets; particular attention is paid in addition to the exchange rate as an important influence on inflation. (See Bank of England, 1983a, 1983b.)

Now, while speculation is no longer explicitly mentioned in conventional monetary theory, it is not denied that it occurs. Indeed, if any mention is made at all of decisions made with respect to the future, it is hard to deny that speculation occurs. The important question is whether it is stabilizing or destabilizing. Friedman (1953) has denied that destabilizing speculation can occur (or at least, that it has been observed to occur – see Friedman, 1970). Any speculator who bought assets as their price rose and sold as their price fell (thus adding destabilizing fuel to price movements) would lose money and be driven out of the market. But if speculation can only be stabilizing, it simply helps to make the market process work more smoothly, ironing out fluctuations occurring for other reasons. Speculation simply helps the economy to reach the long-run equilibrium position it was heading for anyway. Speculation in this sense goes under the name of rational expectations.

We now proceed to discuss speculation in the much broader sense intended by Keynes, and re-examine the way in which monetary policy should be designed if it is to contribute to the stabilization of aggregate demand.

5.3 SPECULATION AND THE LEVEL OF AGGREGATE DEMAND

Speculative behaviour is central to the very idea of capitalism. But most textbooks underplay this crucial point; they depict demand and cost curves as if they are objective, perfectly known features. In a capitalist economy entrepreneurs make profits by hiring factors and purchasing raw materials in the present, and selling outputs of goods and services derived from them for a higher revenue at a later date. Entrepreneurs may know what their present outlays are – on stocks, fixed capital and wages advanced to workers – but they will usually be rather uncertain as to the total output these outlays will generate. They will be even less sure at what prices they will be able to sell particular volumes of output in the future; their demand curve exists only in their imagination as a set of forecasts based on hunches they have about the market conditions. No amount of information on *past* sales will provide certain knowledge about the future. If their guesses turn out to be wrong they may find themselves bankrupt: making losses, not profits.

The inherently unknowable nature of the future forced Keynes (1936, especially ch. 12) to ask from where entrepreneurs got their confidence to invest. His answer was that much depended on the 'state of the news', on psychologically fluid 'animal spirits', and on observations of how other entrepreneurs were behaving. Entrepreneurial behaviour from this standpoint is seen as based on exceedingly flimsy conjectural foundations and interactions between diverse opinions. It can be prone to sudden changes of direction as the state of the news causes shifts in confidence. Shackle describes investment behaviour as inherently *kaleidoscopic* (referring to the child's toy, the kaleidoscope, where slight movements can produce dramatic changes in multi-coloured patterns observed through a peep-hole). Another analogy, suggested by Coddington (1976) in the light of Shackle and Keynes, is of behaviour during riots – demonstrators taking their cues from each other and from a few opinion leaders.

Entrepreneurs are continually on edge because they are afraid of making losses by sinking money into assets with poor income flows and secondhand values vastly below the price they have paid for them. When they are pessimistic they hold on to their money, foregoing the slim prospects they perceive of profits in order to avoid the possibility of capital loss.

Very much the same predicament is faced by consumers. They are also confronted with an unknowable future and the possibility that they will buy the wrong things and thus make costly mistakes. The demand curves imagined by entrepreneurs may fit reality very poorly if consumer choice, too, is highly contingent upon flimsy, shifting expectations and crowd behaviour. Expenditure can dry up suddenly or explode into a consumer boom on the basis of mere shifts in consumer confidence and snippets of news.

For example, if rumours are in the air suggesting that I might lose my job, I will be foolish if I commit myself to regular hire purchase payments on a new car, whose capital value falls by hundreds of pounds the moment I drive it out of the showroom. And if I, for reasons of pessimism, cut down my expenditure on items of conspicuous consumption, my neighbours will not need to spend so much either to preserve their positions of relative status. We all simply drive round in rather older cars and attempt to keep more money in our bank and building society accounts, or reduce the extent of our indebtedness. The flow of expenditure dries up, even if nothing has happened to the money supply; the velocity of circulation declines. But because expenditure has fallen, incomes and employment will fall. Redundant car workers do not have money in their bank accounts to spend, because I have immobilized it in my account, or have failed to increase my indebtedness to a financial institution. My fears of redundancy cause redundancy for others, and may indeed turn out to be self-fulfilling.

This kaleidoscopic view of consumer demand is one to which we may adhere not merely on the basis of armchair theorizing but also in the light of empirical work by Katona (1960, 1976) and Smith (1975). Katona's work shows a close relationship between shifts in consumers' confidence in the ability of their governments to manage the economies in which they live (his 1976 study looks at OECD countries) and shifts in the level of consumer investment, that is expenditure on durable goods. Smith's study of the US car market shows that the demand for cars was highly unstable and related more to changes in confidence than the age of cars or availability of hire purchase finance.

As far as matters of monetary policy are concerned, this view of entrepreneurs and consumers suggests it may be foolish to believe, as monetarists do, that there is a direct link running from the volume of money in the economy (on some arbitrary definition) to the volume of aggregate demand. In a world of speculative economic behaviour, any close relationship between the quantity of money and the quantity of nominal expenditure may be explained by a reverse mechanism of causation, a mechanism which happens also to make the velocity of circulation *appear* stable. This reverse mechanism is as follows. A decline in the desire to spend leads to a smaller growth in the money supply than would otherwise have occurred, because the supply of money responds passively to the demand for it. For example, if I decide not to buy a car, I will not need to increase my overdraft with my bank; the same situation arises with a company which does not borrow to finance an investment scheme because it has decided not to carry it out. The bank, in consequence, will simply be less heavily loaned up than it might have been.

Thus, within a speculative environment, expenditure may not be a stable function either of the money supply or of interest rates. So controlling either will not have a predictable effect on inflation. Even if it has been observed in the past to be related to the money supply or interest rates, it cannot be concluded that a change in either will *cause* a change in expenditure.

5.4 SPECULATION AND INTEREST RATES

In Keynes's analysis of monetary theory, interest rates are depicted as being held where they are at present because holders of monetary assets expect interest rates to be elsewhere in the future.

According to Keynes's speculative motive, individuals who hold wealth in the form of cash do so because they expect the rate of interest to rise and security prices to fall: others who decide instead to hold government stocks do not believe interest rates are going to fall. The balance of opinion determines the rate of interest. But the opinions are contradictory; someone has to be wrong; someone will wish, after the event, that they had taken the other position.

Since interest rates and security prices are held where they are because some people expect that they are going to change, any failure of interest rates to shift in the expected direction will, sooner or later, cause some of the speculators to revise their opinions. If someone is staying out of bonds because they expect interest rates to rise, a tendency for interest rates *not* to rise will suggest that their expectation is incorrect. If they, and others, conclude that interest rates are instead probably going to fall, the natural course of action will be to get out of cash and buy government bonds. The extra demand for bonds will cause their prices to rise and interest rates to fall, confirming the expectations of those who bought the bonds, but falsifying the expectations of other speculators.

Once more, then, we have a vision of speculation and fears of capital losses, set against hopes of capital gains, tending to make markets inherently unstable. Once more, this is in sharp contrast to the prevailing monetarist wisdom. Let us now consider what insights Keynes's view of interest rates gives us in respect of monetary policy.

In Keynes's theory attention is focussed on money which is being used for speculation. People hoard money, either as cash or in bank deposits, because they are afraid of the risks of committing themselves to physical and financial assets. This causes asset prices to be lower than otherwise might be the case, and makes the issue of new securities and the creation of new physical assets less attractive. It is not that the money does not exist to finance more expenditure; it is simply that a lack of confidence deters people with holdings of wealth from lending it to others who would like to carry out the expenditure. The government, by manipulating the 'state of the news', may be able to bring about a shift of confidence. If so, it will be able to finance increased expenditure by selling new government bonds without bringing about any rise in the rate of interest, despite not also increasing the money supply. A government which increases its borrowing simultaneously with announcing that it will take steps to ensure that interest rates do not rise in consequence (for example, by saying that the Bank of England will stand ready to purchase stocks to stabilize interest rates) will find a ready market for its new issue of bonds.

In monetarist theories of interest rates, the emphasis is on money being held for future transactions purposes or to meet contingent expenditure needs (for example, due to illness or redundancy) – that is, for financing likely expenditure – rather than as a speculative hedge for avoiding losses in the value of wealth. It is as if all money is already tied up in expenditure schemes, as if some kind of full employment prevails in money markets. On this view, a government can only sell stocks to finance increased expenditure by bidding money, *which otherwise would have been spent*, away from other uses, by offering a higher rate of return. This is known as 'crowding out'.

The crowding out idea might seem quite plausible to anyone who thinks of 'people who hold money' as private individuals, who do not normally speculate on money markets because any prospects of higher returns than they can obtain from deposit accounts in banks or building societies would be swamped by brokers' fees. But the vast bulk of financial wealth is owned by institutions – corporations, pension funds, insurance companies – who can, by trading on a large scale, overcome the barriers to financial speculation normally posed by brokers' charges, and who can focus their attention on the detailed events in the City of London in a way which is impossible for the ordinary worker. And, by well-conceived attempts to manipulate the expectations of managers of these institutions, governments may be able to finance reflationary spending schemes without having to increase the money supply and without having to allow a rise in interest rates to draw idle bank deposits into an active financial role.

Once more, our analysis also leads us to see no necessary

relationship between the size of some definition of the money supply and the level of nominal aggregate demand; account must be taken of the level of confidence, how willing 'people' are to exchange money for assets of uncertain resale value.

If the economy is in a highly pessimistic state, attempts by the Bank of England to engineer a monetary expansion, and hence promote higher aggregate demand, may be relatively ineffectual. If the Bank makes it known that it will lend to clearing banks on more favourable terms than hitherto, the latter may be rather unwilling to take advantage of this easing in their ability to create credit. Already they may be less than fully loaned up because they cannot see any more creditworthy potential customers in the group of would-be borrowers. There is little point in lending if you do not expect to get the money back and if attempts to reduce the damage a default would cause, by asking for yet higher interest rates, might merely make the default all the more likely. And, on the customers' side of the loan, there is little point in attempting to borrow if the prospect of disaster looms large: a small reduction in interest rates makes the scale of the disaster smaller to a borrower whose income flow, for whatever reason, dries up, but the disaster of not being able to keep up the payments occurs nonetheless. Hence, in pessimistic times the queue of would-be new borrowers may be reduced to the ranks of the financially foolish. Thus, the money multiplier is unlikely to be a stable function of the rate of interest.

But, just as attempts to stimulate new bank lending may make little impact in a period of pessimistic stagnation, so attempts by the Bank of England to prevent expenditure by a monetary squeeze may be doomed to fail if people are determined to spend. If the Bank tightens the terms on which it makes funds available to clearing banks, the latter may still be perfectly willing to expand their overdraft facilities, despite the greater cost, and find willing takers. Where bank financing forms only a small part of the total financial outlay in respect of a particular scheme, it may still be worth borrowing to finance it, even after a high rise in interest rates, because the opportunity cost is so high. In a situation where activity is declining, the marginal returns to a loan can be very high indeed if the alternative is the break up of a company in bankruptcy.

In the past two years the Monetary Authorities' failure to give any weight to this aspect of monetary economics has led them to drive up interest rates in attempts to reduce the growth of the money supply, only to find that this makes it harder for companies to finance their operations: rising interest charges force them to borrow more, not less, in many cases, and so the money supply expands. The demands of companies for funds for 'distress borrowing' are also enhanced by a drying up of informally provided 'trade-credit': as companies get worried about their customers' abilities to pay, they reduce the time span over which they are allowed to meet their bills. This forces companies further along the chain to behave similarly – at some point some firm has either to borrow more from a bank, or to contract the scale of its purchasing, passing the buck back along the chain and increasing the financial difficulties of supplying companies.

Thus, although the authorities have chosen to implement monetary control via interest rates, it has not proved to be effective. The demand for money has not proved to be a stable function of the rate of interest. In the last section, the 'speculative' approach was seen to cast doubt on the stability of the money supply–expenditure relationship: here we have extended that doubt to the money demand–interest-rate relationship.

5.5 SPECULATION AND COMPETITIVE BANKING

The foregoing difficulties of using interest rates to control the demand for money and thus aggregate spending have, in the past two years, led to suggestions that the money supply be controlled more directly. Among other things, this would require that the 'Lender of Last Resort' role of the Bank should be phased out (see Dow, 1982). Banks should be constrained in their lending by their cash ratios alone. If an individual bank wished to expand its private sector lending, and was already fully loaned up, it would have to bid against other banks for cash reserves, trading in government bonds for cash. This would tend to cause a fall in bond prices and a rise in the rate of interest. If the Bank of England were no longer to step in as a purchaser of bonds to stabilize their prices, interest rates would have to find their own level. The idea is that if there were strict control over the volume of cash in the system, changes in the scale of overdrafts provided by clearing banks to financially hard-pressed customers would take the form of loans made at the expense of other customers, not new loans made possible by accommodating lending by the Bank of England.

Minsky's (1976) development of Keynes's ideas leads us to suspect that such a policy, ruthlessly applied, would comprise a recipe for disaster. Minsky emphasizes that modern financial systems are multi-layered debt structures – a point which should already be apparent following our discussion of trade credit chains – and the ability to borrow of any element in these systems is heavily dependent on the perceived value of its collateral. If a wave of pessimism sweeps over an economy asset prices will tend to fall – the price of shares on the stock market, for example, will fall as expectations of dividends are revised downwards – and so, too, will expenditure. Since this reduction in expenditure will only have been anticipated imperfectly, some firms will be left with unsold stocks to finance and will need to borrow more to stave off bankruptcy. But the willingness of 'people' to lend will be falling too. Would-be borrowers may, because of the collapse of asset values and expectations of future income flows, be unable to arrange loans and consequently, go bankrupt.

Financial layering means that bankruptcies at one level promote further bankruptcies, and a further scramble for finance to prevent them. Rising interest rates must be the upshot of such a scramble, but they will only exacerbate the problem by reducing asset prices and the value of possible loan collateral still further.

Some indication of Minsky's analysis at work is given by the behaviour of the British property market in 1973–5, and the effects it had on the City of London. In the 1972–3 boom, excessive confidence in the ability of property to provide a hedge against inflation had caused a massive rise in property prices, for the supply of property was relatively fixed. Property firms found the values of their assets rising and used them as collateral against loans to finance further purchases of property. These loans were provided by 'secondary banks', less reliable institutions than clearing banks, which had been able to attract deposits or borrow relatively cheaply on the 'London Interbank Market' as a result of the state of high confidence.

When the property boom came to an end in the pessimism of the Yom Kippur War and with the rise in oil prices at the end of 1973, property prices fell. Since rental earnings could not pay for interest on debts incurred by the property firms, they had to sell off their assets instead. No longer could they use capital gains to meet financing charges in excess of rental yields. Asset sales merely exacerbated the situation. Some property companies failed and this cast doubt on the capital adequacy of the secondary banks (some of whom are 'incestuously' linked with particular property firms), causing a withdrawal of deposits. Secondary banks, too, thus found themselves facing collapse. The plague of failures even threatened to spread itself to the big clearing banks. For a time, the shares of the National Westminster Bank fell below par – something unheard of in such a bank – because of its involvement with the failed London and Counties Securities group. The cumulating collapse was only stopped by the Bank of England stepping in with a financial 'lifeboat' of loans, which aimed to reduce the rate of liquidation of failed firms' assets and thereby to limit the extent of the collapse in asset prices. But the delay in the Bank's Lender of Last Resort action had already enabled a substantial catalogue of failure to accumulate (see further Dow and Earl, 1982, ch. 12).

The Bank of England responded to this experience by extending its supervisory role over a broad range of financial institutions, under the Banking Act of 1979. A series of consultative documents was also issued with proposals for influencing the portfolios of the entire range of deposit-taking institutions, to ensure solvency. (See Dow, 1982.)

The financial chaos of the mid-1970s occurred after the Competition and Credit Control regulations of a few years before had allowed the 'free entry' of precisely those kinds of institutions which failed. It occurred even despite there being no policy decision to prevent the Bank of England from stepping in rapidly with funds to support asset prices. With an effectively passive Central Bank, the free market's unguided search for an equilibrium level of interest rates, in a situation where confidence had completely collapsed, could have dealt a fatal blow to the international credibility of London as a financial centre. A collapse of confidence in the system as a whole, now that foreign exchange controls have been removed, could also lead to a massive outflow of foreign funds and an inflationary collapse of sterling's international value. Free market banking, an absence of foreign exchange controls, and a commitment of the authorities against intervention in a disequilibrium situation would leave the financial sector – perhaps even the economy as a whole – in an extremely vulnerable position.

The 1979 Banking Act represents an attempt to forestall such a situation. But, although monetary base control as such was not in fact implemented, the freer competition it attempted to promote is still cause for concern. Competition is only effective when the threat of bankruptcy is real; and bankruptcy within the financial sector can have very damaging consequences.

In this section, therefore, we have demonstrated the dangers involved in controlling the money supply itself or indeed of any rigid system of control – dangers recognised by the Bank of England (1983a). An *effective* system of control would lead to failures of financial institutions, which could lead to the collapse of the financial system itself.

5.6 CONCLUSION

The introduction of a speculative perspective into monetary economics leaves the Keynesian theorist alarmed at the likely outcome of policies developed from the standpoint of a world view that is blind to the destabilizing potential of financial speculation. But the existence of speculators – and we ourselves as consumers, with our discretion in the timing of purchases of durable goods, must count amongst the ranks of speculators – raises fundamental questions about how the economy should be managed.

The scope for changes in 'the news' to send the economy lurching off discontinuously in different directions means that demand management should be alert to the 'mood' of the economy as much as to measured relationships based on past experience. Second, institutions (particularly in the financial sector) should be designed to limit as far as possible the destabilizing effects of speculative shifts. Third, both monetary and fiscal policy should be implemented in such a way as not to *cause* destabilizing speculative shifts (which would undermine the effectiveness of policy).

In terms of monetary policy, then, the capacity to promote a steady growth of aggregate demand without destabilizing financial developments would be enhanced by the following measures:

1   The money supply should be allowed to grow in line with the demand for finance; that is, monetary policy should be passive, but passive in the reverse of the sense entailed in present non-interventionist thinking. The Lender of Last Resort should lend on demand and not attempt to manipulate interest rates.
2   No attempt should be made to control expenditure by manipulation of interest rates. Small shifts in interest rates are ineffectual in promoting increases or reductions in the level of expenditure. Large shifts, because of their effects on asset values, are liable to be fiercely powerful (that is, a big increase in interest rates, to reduce the growth of expenditure, will cause a big fall in asset values and a speculative collapse instead of the intended moderate reduction).
3   Foreign exchange controls should be reintroduced to prevent divergences between (stable) domestic interest rates and overseas interest rates from causing destabilizing currency flows and exchange rate movements.
4   Entry into the business of banking should be carefully controlled, followed up by close supervision.

At present, fiscal policy is subservient to monetary policy, with public sector borrowing limited to allow monetary targets to be met. Having demonstrated the difficulties attached to an 'active' monetary policy, we propose that fiscal policy be the main vehicle for demand management. Fiscal policy within a speculative environment must take account of the role of expectations in influencing private sector expenditure plans. Thus the *awareness* of the existence of the social security system acting as a cushion encourages more stable spending patterns when the employment future is uncertain; this fact itself, by bolstering aggregate demand reduces actual social security expenditure. More generally, the *presentation* of fiscal policy is as important as its content. In wartime as in 'Buy British' campaigns it has been demonstrated that individuals are not selfish economic automatons but are open to persuasion to act in what they are persuaded to perceive as the social interest. This is a fact of political life. It is the task of economists to suggest what policies, given the range of possible social goals, are in fact in the public interest.

REFERENCES

Bank of England (1983a) 'Setting Money Objectives', *Bank of England Quarterly Bulletin*, 23, June, pp. 200–8.

(1983b) 'The Bank's Operational Procedures for Meeting Monetary Objectives', *Bank of England Quarterly Bulletin*, 23, June, pp. 201–15.

Baumol, W. J. (1952) 'The Transactions Demand for Cash: An Inventory Theoretic Approach', *Quarterly Journal of Economics*, 66, November, pp. 545–56.

Coddington, A. (1976) 'Keynesian Economics: The Search for First Principles', *Journal of Economic Literature*, 14, December, pp. 1258–73.

Dow, S. C. (1982) 'Recent Developments in UK Monetary Policy', *Stirling Economics Teaching Paper No. 8*. University of Stirling, Department of Economics, February.

Dow, S. C. and Earl, P. E. (1982) *Money Matters: A Keynesian Approach to Monetary Economics* (Oxford: Martin Robertson).

Friedman, M. (1953) 'The Case for Flexible Exchange Rates', in *Essays in Positive Economics* (Chicago: Chicago University Press).

(1970) 'Discussion of C. P. Kindleberger, The Case for Fixed Exchange Rates, 1969', in Federal Reserve Bank of Boston, *The International Adjustment Mechanism,* Boston, pp. 114–15.

HMSO (1980) *Monetary Control*, Cmnd 7858.

Katona, G. (1960) *The Powerful Consumer: Psychological Studies of the American Economy* (New York: McGraw-Hill).

Katona, G. (1976) 'Consumer Investment Versus Business Investment', *Challenge*, January/February.

Keynes, J. M. (1936) *The General Theory Of Employment, Interest and Money* (London: Macmillan).

Minsky, H. P. (1976) *John Maynard Keynes* (London: Macmillan).

Shackle, G. L. S. (1974) *Keynesian Kaleidics* (Edinburgh: Edinburgh University Press).

Smith, R. P. (1975) *Consumer Demand for Cars in the USA* (Cambridge: Cambridge University Press).

Tobin, J. (1958) 'Liquidity Preference as Behaviour Towards Risk', *Review of Economic Studies*, 25, February, 65–86.

Useful additional articles in bank reviews

Cramp, A. B. (1970) 'Does Money Matter?' *Lloyds Bank Review*, No. 98, October, pp. 23–37.

Kaldor, N. (1970) 'The New Monetarism', *Lloyds Bank Review*, No. 97, July, pp. 1–18.

Kaldor, N. and Trevithick, J. (1981) 'A Keynesian Perspective on Money', *Lloyds Bank Review*, No. 139, January, pp. 1–19.

Lewis, M. (1980) 'Rethinking Monetary Policy', *Lloyds Bank Review*, No. 137, July, pp. 41–60.

Tew, J. H. B. (1981) 'The Implementation of Monetary Policy in Post-War Britain', *Midland Bank Review*, Spring, pp. 5–14.

QUESTIONS FOR DISCUSSION

1 'Whilst the weakening of credit is sufficient to bring about a collapse, its strengthening, though a necessary condition of recovery, is not a sufficient condition' (J. M. Keynes (1936), p. 158). Discuss.

2 'Demand depends not merely upon a consumer's ability to spend, but also upon her willingness.' Discuss the complications this causes for attempts to manage demand by monetary means.

3 Is the level of spending determined by the level of the money supply, or is the level of the money supply determined by the level of spending? In your answer, be careful to explain what you mean by 'the money supply'.

4 What is the money multiplier? In what way(s) is it influenced by the rate of interest?

5 Why is the speculative demand for money usually expressed as a negative function of the rate of interest? Are there any circumstances where the speculative demand for money might rise even though the rate of interest had not fallen?

6 What factors might explain a negative relationship between the demand for money and the rate of interest, other than the speculative demand for money?

7 Why do we assume that actual money holdings (the money supply) represents the demand for money?

8 'Changes in the quantity of money affect interest rates rather than prices.' Discuss.

9 What are the functions of money? How does the government limit the amount of money that banks are able to provide?

10 'Monetary policy is preferable to fiscal policy as a means of controlling the economy because it is less discriminatory.' Discuss.

11 How are interest rates determined?

6 British Exchange Rate Policy

RONALD SHONE

Under the Bretton Woods system of exchange rate management, the policy of the British government towards the exchange rate was constrained. Besides intervening to contain the rate within specified limits, the only policy issue was whether and when to change the peg rate (this was a question of devaluation in the British case). This system collapsed in 1971 and from 1973 was replaced by a system of generalized floating. Under this system the policy towards the exchange rate is not so clear.

In the first section we shall outline the major developments since 1945, and then turn in the second section to attitudes towards the exchange rate over the same period. In the third section we consider the causal links between inflation, unemployment and the exchange rate. In the final section we turn to the question of whether, under a floating exchange rate system, the UK should have an exchange rate policy.

6.1 HISTORICAL OVERVIEW

The Bretton Woods system was set up in 1944 to avoid three major problems which typified the interwar period, namely (1) to avoid competitive devaluations, (2) to avoid exchange and trade restrictions, and (3) to deal with the lack of international reserves. In simple terms this system involved each country expressing its exchange rate at a fixed rate in terms of the dollar (called the parity rate), the dollar in turn to be held fixed in terms of gold. For the foreign exchange markets to function, exchange rates were allowed to move 1 per cent either side of their par values. In addition the International Monetary Fund (IMF) was set up to oversee the system and to deal with the issues of international liquidity and competitive exchange rate changes. In Britain this system became fully operative after 1958 . when sterling became freely convertible for the first time.

It is worth mentioning at this point that 'convertibility' has two distinct meanings which do not have to operate at the same time – a point of significance in the breakdown of the Bretton Woods system. The two uses of convertibility are:

(i)   market convertibility
(ii)   official convertibility.

The first refers to the act of freely converting one currency into another, while the second refers to the act of a central bank converting dollars into gold at the official rate. When both operate, then the system is linked to gold, while if the first only operates then the system is linked (usually) only to the dollar and not necessarily to gold.

Under the Bretton Woods system, a parity value was set for the spot exchange rate (no such control was placed on the forward exchange rate). The spot exchange rate is the rate at which one

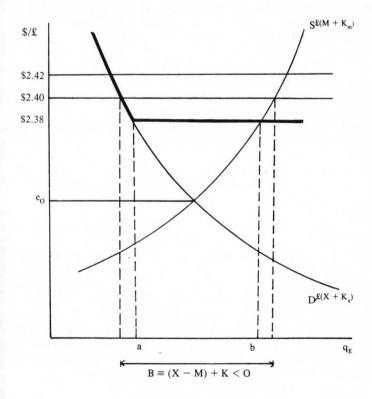

Figure 6.1   Bretton Woods system

currency is exchanged for another for immediate delivery (in practice, within two working days). It was this market rate which could fluctuate 1 per cent either side of the agreed parity rate. For example, after the 1967 devaluation of sterling the parity rate was £1 = $2.40 with a margin of fluctuation of ±2 cents, that is, a range for the market rate of $2.42 to $2.38 (Note that the British express the exchange rate as the foreign price of sterling while other countries express their rate as the domestic price of the foreign currency.) The forward rate of exchange arises from contracts which fix the price now for the future purchase or delivery of a currency. Although the IMF placed no restriction on the fluctuations in the forward rate, individual countries did intervene in this market from time to time. For instance, during the 1964 crisis, and again in the crisis of 1967, the Bank of England intervened quite significantly in the forward market.

In fact, intervention occurred in both the spot and the forward market. It is crucial to appreciate this since it highlights a major difficulty in operating the Bretton Woods system and indicates why a number of economists suggested a floating exchange rate. To understand the mechanics of intervention consider Figure 6.1. The demand for sterling arises from the export of British goods and services along with the export of capital (note: the securities are exported but the money flows into Britain), while the supply of sterling arises from imports of goods and services and the import of capital (here we refer only to short term capital).

Under a truly freely floating exchange rate with quick adjustment the exchange rate would settle down at the equilibrium rate e_0. However, suppose the rate is fixed at, say £1 = $2.40 (±2 cents). The first thing we notice in terms of the curves as drawn is that the equilibrium rate cannot be achieved. Second, at the fixed parity rate of £1 = $2.40 Britain has a deficit on its balance of payments, since at this rate we have

$$B = (X - M) + K < O$$

that is, a deficit on the current plus capital account (where X = exports, M = imports, so $X - M$ is the current balance; and K is the net balance on capital account).

The market rate can fall to £1 = $2.38 but cannot, under the rules of the system, fall below this level. But how is this brought about? At $2.38 the Bank of England must step in and demand sterling. What this means is that the demand curve for sterling becomes infinitely elastic at this value. Given the market demand and supply of sterling, this means that the Bank must demand £ab of sterling. In demanding sterling it must supply something in exchange – it must supply gold or dollars in exchange, in the present case $2.38 × ab. Thus a deficit on

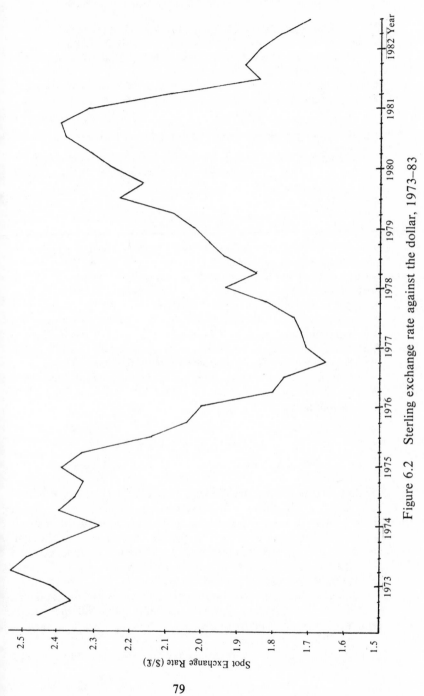

Figure 6.2   Sterling exchange rate against the dollar, 1973–83

tha balance of payments leads to a loss of foreign exchange reserves while a surplus leads to a rise in a country's foreign exchange reserves.

What happens when a country has a persistent deficit, as was the case for Britain? The analysis indicates that it will persistently lose some of its reserves. If the reserves get dangerously low, then two other courses of action are open to the government:

(1) borrow abroad (either from another country or from the IMF)
(2) devalue its exchange rate.

In practice the first has usually been followed. However, when the borrowing became excessive and the loss of reserves too great (as in 1967), then devaluation is the only course of action left under the Bretton Woods system.

For a variety of reasons the Bretton Woods system came under great pressure at the end of the 1960s. It came to a head in 1971 when President Nixon broke the link between the dollar and gold (that is, he suspended official convertibility). A period of turmoil ensued with a variety of attempts to patch up the system. In the meantime Britain had floated sterling in June 1972. Originally this was to be a temporary measure but like so many temporary measures instituted by governments, this is still with us. Since the floating of sterling there was a depreciation vis-à-vis the dollar, reaching a low point in 1976. This was followed by an appreciation, reaching a peak in 1980. Since then the dollar/pound exchange rate has once again depreciated. This is shown rather dramatically in Figure 6.2. As we shall discuss later, both depreciation and appreciation have led to difficulties for the British economy.

6.2 POST-WAR POLICIES TOWARDS THE EXCHANGE RATE

In simple terms the Bretton Woods system can be thought of as a fixed exchange-rate system which allowed infrequent discrete changes in parity rates. Since 1972 Britain can be considered to be under a floating exchange-rate system. Neither, of course, occur in the pure form so often discussed in textbooks but these two extremes – fixed versus floating exchange rates – do highlight the essential differences between the two systems in practice.

Under the Bretton Woods system the policy towards the exchange rate was to maintain the fixed parity rate with only small fluctuations either side, as we outlined in the first section. Generally, the parity rate was treated as sacrosanct. Even in 1964 when the accumulated deficit on the balance of payments was very large, the outgoing

Conservative government refrained from devaluation and the incoming Labour government (under Harold Wilson) made 'no devaluation' a party pledge. The point about this period was that a fixed rate had become a sign of government 'success', and whether it was economically sound to devalue took second place.

Because of this insistence on maintaining a parity rate in the face of growing deficits, the British economy had to adjust in other directions. One typical adjustment was to cut back aggregate demand. This reduced the level of income, which in turn reduced the value of imports (since imports are linked to income via the marginal propensity to import). Thus the 1950s and 1960s were characterized by typical 'stop-go' policies, expanding the economy when the balance of payments was in surplus and contracting the economy when it was in deficit.

One other adjustment was open to the government which can be appreciated with the aid of Figure 6.1. We see from Figure 6.1 that

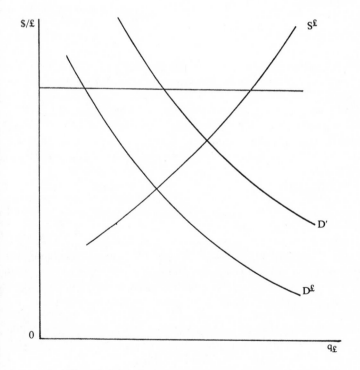

Figure 6.3   Rise in British interest rates

short-term capital enters both schedules. Short-term capital responds
very much to interest rates: capital exports respond to British interest
rates and capital imports to US interest rates (net capital flows are
therefore dependent on the interest rate differential). Suppose Britain
is in deficit, as shown in Figure 6.3. If Britain raises its interest rates,
then the demand curve for sterling shifts to the right, to D^1. This in
turn raises the equilibrium market exchange rate, and under a fixed
exchange rate system reduces the size of the deficit on the balance of
payments (although not on the current account). This solution is one
of raising capital inflows to finance the current account deficit.

It is of course possible to impose import controls – as Harold
Wilson did in 1964. This too will reduce the deficit, but in this case by
dealing with the current account.

We see, then, that we have a number of policy options for
improving the balance of payments which can be used singly or in
combination. These are:

1   devalue the exchange rate
2   reduce the level of income
3   raise interest rates
4   impose import controls.

Up to 1972 all of these were tried, but the exchange rate was devalued
only twice in the post-war period: first in 1949 and again in 1967. By
1972 the world situation was such that a sterling float seemed the best
option.

With a freely floating exchange rate, and a quick adjustment in the
foreign exchange market, then (according to textbooks) there would
be no need for foreign exchange reserves since there would not be a
balance of payments deficit or surplus. Any such tendency towards a
deficit or surplus would lead to immediate changes in the market
exchange rate and to their elimination. The exchange rate would
move up or down in order to equilibrate demand and supply. In such a
situation no policy towards the exchange rate is called for. Has this
been borne out by practice?

In Table 6.1 we record the balance of payments on current account
and the negative of official financing (equal to the current balance plus
net capital flows plus the balancing item). As shown by this table there
has not been an elimination of deficits or surpluses. Even when we
take a five-year cumulative total it still appears that deficits and
surpluses occur.

Leaving aside the difficulties in recording balance of payments
figures, this would suggest either that the theory is wrong or that there
has not in fact been free floating since 1972, and that some
intervention ('dirty' floating) has occurred. A look at Figure 6.2 would

Table 6.1   Balance of payments

Year	Current balance		Balance of payments*	
1972	+247		−1141	
1973	−981		−771	
1974	−3273	−6403	−1646	−8651
1975	−1521		−1465	
1976	−875		−3628	
1977	−22		+7361	
1978	+1018		+1126	
1979	−853	+9044	+1710	+8630
1980	+2865		+1372	
1981	+6036		−687	

* This is equal to the current balance plus net capital flows plus the balancing item.

SOURCE: *Economic Trends*, Annual Supplement 1983.

support the view that there has in fact been some intervention in the spot exchange market: that some 'dirty' floating has been undertaken.

During the period 1972–6 there was a deliberate policy to depreciate the exchange rate. This general depreciating trend is clearly shown in Figure 6.2. However, two difficulties arose. First, the government lost control of the rate and it began to fall to a rate lower than they had anticipated. This period highlighted the difficulty of (a) managing the trend rate, and (b) managing the speed of response. Second, the depreciation lowered export prices and raised import prices. Although this improved the balance of payments (after a time lag – the J-curve effect) it also gave a stimulus to the rate of inflation. Not only does Britain have a high marginal propensity to import, but many imports are inputs into British manufactures (including exports). The result was that on average a depreciating pound led to a rise in domestic prices in later years.

After the crisis of 1976 the exchange rate appreciated and a policy of evening out fluctuations in the exchange rate was followed, that is, of 'leaning against the wind'. This has been the policy followed since the Conservative government took office in 1979.

But if a depreciation leads to difficulties, does this mean that an

appreciation is beneficial? An appreciation raises export prices and
lowers import prices. This means that Britain loses out in its
competitive position in world markets. It does mean, however, that
inflation is curbed somewhat, or at least is not fuelled through the
exchange market. Thus, when the exchange rate is appreciating it is
exporters who complain and not the government. This does lead to a
conflict of interests. This conflict became even more apparent when
North Sea Oil began to flow, from about 1979. This lowered Britain's
imports of oil and raised oil exports. The combined effect was to shift
the demand curve for sterling to the right and the supply of sterling to
the left, as shown in Figure 6.4. The result was to raise the exchange
rate.

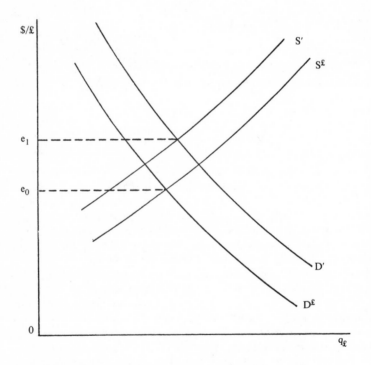

Figure 6.4   The effect of North Sea Oil

Although the present government has no direct policy towards the
trend in the exchange rate (only towards fluctuations around the
trend) it does, all the same, have a definite *indirect* influence on the

trend. To see this, we must return to Figure 6.3. The present government has the overriding objective of reducing inflation. It is achieving this through a restrictive monetary policy and a cut in the Public Sector Borrowing Requirement (PSBR) consistent with it. This has meant a rise in British interest rates. But this will lead to an inflow of capital and so a shift in the demand for sterling to the right. The result of this shift is to raise the exchange rate. Conversely, as interest rates begin to fall, so does the exchange rate, which is also show in Figure 6.2.

One further point is worth making about the exchange rate, which has a bearing on the issue of whether the government should influence the rate. Under the Bretton Woods system we noted that the market exchange rate could fluctuate by 1 per cent either side of the par value.

Table 6.2   Variations in the sterling exchange rate

	Bretton Woods			*Floating*	
Year	Mean	SD	Year	Mean	SD
1963	2.7997	0.0020	1972[c]	2.5437	0.3284
1964	2.7921	0.0060	1973	2.4565	0.0775
1965	2.7962	0.0055	1974	2.3527	0.0429
1966	2.7928	0.0046	1975	2.2078	0.1516
1967[a]	2.7906	0.0058	1976	1.7938	0.1338
1968	2.3923	0.0091	1977	1.7591	0.0622
1969	2.3910	0.0057	1978	1.9320	0.0763
1970	2.3962	0.0079	1979	2.1345	0.0897
1971	2.4503	0.0433	1980	2.3314	0.0736
1972[b]	2.6079	0.0076	1981	2.0163	0.1788
			1982	1.8159	0.0778

a First 10 months. b First 5 months. c Last 7 months.

Note: The mean is the arithmetic average of the monthly rates in each year (or part year). The standard deviation (SD) is a simple measure of the variability of the monthly figures about the mean for the corresponding year.

SOURCE: Bank of England Quarterly Bulletin, various issues.

Under this system, therefore, fluctuations in the exchange rate were not very great. Since floating, however, this has not been the case. In Table 6.2 we present the mean and standard deviation of the monthly spot exchange rate figures for each year, 1962–82. The greater variation in the spot rate is reflected by the growing standard deviation. For many businesses the fluctuations appear to be even larger since they will be influenced by weekly rates – or even daily rates. Such fluctuations are of the major concern to the big multinational companies.

During the Bretton Woods period the major uncertainty for large companies concerned their production levels. Now it would appear that exchange rate uncertainty can be much greater – certainly in terms of its influence on profitability.

6.3 INFLATION, UNEMPLOYMENT AND THE EXCHANGE RATE

One reason to consider having a policy about the exchange rate is because it can, and does, have an influence on inflation and unemployment. But the causal mechanism is not at all clear.

Let us consider first the effect of a depreciation of the exchange rate. This raises import prices and lowers export prices. Although both prices enter the computation of the general price level, the rise in import prices (measured in £-sterling) is usually greater than the fall in export prices (measured in foreign currency) – most especially because imports tend to enter the production of many goods produced in the UK. The result is a rise in the general price level. If the depreciation persists, then there is a definite upward pressure on the rate of inflation. It must also be realized that this influence may take a number of years to be felt.

The depreciation has a beneficial impact on business. The rise in import prices means that goods produced by the import substitute industries become relatively cheaper. Also, because exports now become relatively cheaper, export sales will probably rise. Whether the increased sales lead to an increase in employment depends on the amount of spare capacity that exists. It does not automatically follow that employment will rise as a consequence of the depreciation. The depreciation will have to be significant and persistent for this to be a real possibility.

In the case of an appreciation the argument is reversed. Import prices fall and export prices rise. It does not follow, however, that the general price index will fall. This partly depends on whether the fall in import prices leads to a fall in the price of many of the goods using those imports. It is possible, for instance, that businessmen will simply raise their profit margins to recover from the period when these were reduced. The loss in sales in the import substitute industries and the export industries will lead to pressure on the level of employment. If the appreciation is significant and persistent then the level of employment will most likely fall.

It will be noted that the argument being advanced here involved some asymmetry. A depreciation is likely to lead to higher inflation but only a probable increase in the level of employment. An appreciation is likely to lead to a fall in the level of employment and only a probable decrease in the rate of inflation. If this is true, then even an x per cent depreciation followed by an x per cent appreciation is likely to be inflationary, with a probable net loss in employment. Even with the wide swings in the exchange rate exhibited in Figure 6.2, the overall trend in the rate is downwards. The consequence, then, is pressure on the rate of inflation and a tendency to raise the level of unemployment. Notice, too, that the result is both an increase in inflation and an increase in the level of unemployment – the Phillips trade off between inflation and unemployment does not come into this argument.

The question arises, however, whether the causation does go from the exchange rate to inflation and unemployment. Is the depreciation (or appreciation) simply the result of the economic climate and not the other way around? To see this point, suppose Britain is inflating at a greater rate than her trading partners. This will lead to a decline in exports and a rise in imports. The current account balance will worsen, and, with a freely floating exchange rate, will lead to a depreciation. In this sense the depreciation does not cause the increase in the rate of inflation; it simply reflects the relatively higher British inflation rate. This could certainly account for the depreciation of sterling when it began to float in 1972 until its lowest point in October 1976. For the argument to hold it must also explain the appreciation of sterling from late 1976 to October 1980. To keep the argument brief, the main reason for this lies with the rise in interest rates and, from 1979 onwards, the presence of North Sea Oil. We have already noted in terms of Figure 6.3, that a rise in British interest rates will lead to an increase in the demand for sterling and a consequent appreciation. That North Sea Oil is not the dominating influence is reflected in the fact that the exchange rate depreciated after the end of 1980 even with continued oil production.

This rather complex causation is too often overlooked in arguments about exchange-rate policy. It is possible that both are true. The higher British inflation can lead to a depreciation of sterling, which in turn leads to even higher rates of inflation. If such a vicious circle does arise, then there is an argument for exchange-rate intervention or some other means to break the circle. Whether intervention should be in the domestic market or in the foreign-exchange market is not at all clear. The important point, however, is to break the circular link.

6.4 IS THERE A NEED FOR A POLICY TOWARDS THE EXCHANGE RATE?

This is not an easy question, but this does not mean that we should shy away from attempting an answer. In doing this, however, it is clear that one's political leaning will influence the likely response. For instance, Conservatives tend to be believers in the free market. Their likely response, and certainly the response of the present government, is that the exchange market should be left to itself and the Bank's role that of 'leaning against the wind', that is, simply ironing out fluctuations. But we have just seen that the domestic policy of fighting inflation can itself lead to a rise in the trend rate of exchange. Is this leaving the market to its own devices? The argument about no government intervention makes sense only when the government is not a major participant in the market. But in modern society the government is a major participant in the market. To ignore this fact will always lead to misplaced policy recommendations.

Accepting what has just been said, does this imply that the government should intervene in the foreign exchange market? If we turn to the Labour party they would argue more for import controls and managed trade (not simply a management of the exchange rate). Putting aside import controls, managing the exchange rate can take a variety of forms. Two issues must always be clearly distinguished:

1 Do we want management of the trend exchange rate?
2 Do we wish to manage variations around the trend exchange rate?

Clearly we can have the first but not the second, the second but not the first, both or neither. The present government follows the second but not (directly) the first. To follow a policy of managing the trend rate would require the government to know what rate is consistent with its other policy objectives and the trend in many of the economy's variables. Although a tall order, this is not impossible. The Treasury model of the British economy can be used (and is used) for this purpose. But this in turn depends on what faith you have in large econometric models as a guide to managing the economy. The government's record in fine tuning has not been a resoundingly successful one. But doing something badly does not imply that it should not be done at all!

To conclude on a personal note, it is my contention that the government should intervene to influence the trend rate, and to even out fluctuations about the trend. More than that, I would also argue that they should also disclose their method or criteria for intervention to eliminate some of the undoubted uncertainty that surrounds the foreign-exchange market. Such a policy would certainly help business-men, especially in their future planning.

SUGGESTIONS FOR FURTHER READING

Abbot, A. C. (1979) 'Recent Developments in the International Monetary System and their Implications for International Economic Relations', *Journal of Economic Studies*, May, pp. 129–54.

Batchelor, R. A. and Wood, G. E. (1982) *Exchange Rate Policy* (London: Macmillan).

Blackaby, F. (1980) 'Exchange-Rate Policy and Economic Strategy', *Three Banks Review*, June, pp. 3–17.

Emminger, O. (1979) 'The Exchange Rate as an Instrument of Economic Policy', *Lloyds Bank Review*, July, pp. 1–22.

Grubel, H. G. (1977) *The International Monetary System*, 3rd ed. (Harmondsworth: Penguin Books).

Hirsch, F. and Higham, D. (1974) 'Floating Exchange Rates: Expectations and Experience', *Three Banks Review*, June.

Major, R. (ed.) (1979) *Britain's Trade and Exchange-Rate Policy* (London: Heinemann).

Midland Bank (1981) 'A Return to Bretton Woods?', *Midland Bank Review*, Autumn/Winter, pp. 30–4.

Oppenheimer, P. *et al.* (1978) *Business Views on Exchange Rate Policy*, (London: CBI).

Shone, R. *et al.* (1978) *Lectures on UK Balance of Payments*, Economic Association.

Tew, B. (1977) *The Evolution of the International Monetary System 1945–77* (London: Hutchinson).

Williamson, J. (1977) *The Failure of World Monetary Reform, 1971–74* (London: Nelson).

Wood, G. E. (1981) 'Do Exchange Rates Overshoot?', *The Banker*, May.

QUESTIONS FOR DISCUSSION

1 Can intervention in the foreign exchange market make things worse? How and why?
2 Why has the present government chosen not to intervene in determining the trend exchange rate?
3 If volatility is reduced in the foreign exchange market by

government intervention, will this result in greater volatility elsewhere in the economy?

4   Theory indicates that in a freely floating exchange rate system the change in reserves will be zero. Table 6.1 indicates this is not true in practice. Reconcile these differences.

5   Who gains and who loses by a depreciation (appreciation) of sterling?

6   Have floating exchange rates removed the problem of balance-of-payments adjustment?

7   Can floating exchange rates be inflationary?

8   Was the collapse of the Bretton Woods system inevitable?

9   'Under a fixed exchange rate system, changes in the exchange rate led to J-curve effects. Under a floating exchange rate the problem is under or overshooting.' Explain.

10 Argue for or against an exchange-rate target.

Part II
MICROECONOMIC POLICY

7 Industrial Policy in Britain

MAURICE KIRBY

7.1 THE NATURE OF BRITISH INDUSTRIAL WEAKNESS

One of the most depressing features of British economic development during the last hundred years has been the progressive inability of industry to compete both at home and abroad. From the late nineteenth century onwards, apart from relatively brief respites during the 1930s and late 1940s and the period of the two world wars, the status of the industrial sector of the economy has been steadily undermined as foreign competitors have outstripped British firms in their production, productivity and technological records. In the generation before 1914 the growing import penetration of the domestic market by German and American enterprise resulted in a reassessment of Britain's international economic position which was ultimately reflected in the Conservative party's espousal of imperial tariff protection. Such a system was eventually introduced in the 1930s and its progressive dismantlement in the 1950s and 1960s, in accordance with the post-war liberalization of trade and payments, was followed in the mid-1970s by renewed calls for import controls. The latter development was an inevitable by-product of a heightened awareness of British industrial deficiencies in the aftermath of the oil crisis of 1973 when imports of foreign manufactures reached unprecedented levels. 'De-industrialization' – a convenient term to describe the erosion of the industrial base – came to be a major topic of discussion among economists, and although diagnoses and policy prescriptions for reversing Britain's relative decline as a manufacturing nation differed the debate was an open manifestation of the coexistence of chronic and acute problems in the industrial sector. (See Kirby, 1981.)

The term 'inability to compete' covers a multitude of sins and a vast literature has emerged in the last two decades which has attempted to analyse the causes of British industrial weakness. The most widely

accepted diagnoses suggest that the productive efficiency of industry
has been seriously impaired by the lack of professionalism of British
management combined with structural weaknesses in the trade union
movement which have led to overmanning and the perpetuation of
restrictive practices. Similar analyses have drawn attention to Britain's
anachronistic social structure which has encouraged labour unrest by
promoting divisive attitudes in industry, to deficiencies in the
educational system which have led to an overly 'academic' bias at the
expense of the vocational needs of industry, and to a 'contempt for
production' as a result of a myopic concern with macro-economic
issues – itself the product of a Treasury-dominated civil service elite
and the predilection of academic economists for theoretical studies
with limited application to the real economy. The theme which is
common to all of these factors is perhaps more cultural than
economic, being related to the values and assumptions inherited from
Britain's imperial past and former 'great power' status.[1] Indeed, an
excellent case can be made for emphasizing the deleterious effects of
this historical legacy. Faced by mounting foreign competition from
the late nineteenth century onwards 'the first industrial nation'
retreated into empire and latterly Commonwealth markets. These
were characterized by a relatively low preference for manufactured
goods of high unit value, and the protective arrangements referred to
above bred attitudes of complacency and arrogance which served the
country ill when an outmoded industrial structure was exposed to the
full force of international competition after the mid-1950s. (See
Walker, 1980, pp. 19–37.)

At a more detailed level there have been criticisms of the
inappropriateness of government policy in the micro sphere – the
excessive concentration of state-sponsored research and development
(R and D) expenditures on nuclear power, civil aviation and defence,
the inconsistency of policy over time as the institutions created by one
administration were abolished by another, and the long neglect of the
innovative capacity of small firms in the face of an undue preference
for large-scale organizations. Finally, much has been made of the
relatively low level of investment in manufacturing industry leading to
a slow rate of adaptation to technological change and market demand
– all of this compounded by the inept pattern of industrial funding with
a preference in the mechanical engineering industry, for example, for
investment in static technologies leading to a cumulative failure to
keep in step with a constantly changing international technological
frontier in terms of best practice techniques.[2]

It should be stressed that this is by no means an exhaustive list of
the alleged reasons for weak industrial performance. Other factors
would include the lack of competition over wide sectors of industry,

the deadweight of an inefficient nationalized sector and the harmful effects on the productive base of the economy of excessive expansion in public sector services. These are important and central areas of concern and are therefore the subject of separate treatment elsewhere in this volume. Even so, the above catalogue of inadequacies has been the subject of searching inquiry to the extent that it has established the framework for much of the discussion of government industrial policy in the last two decades.

7.2 INDUSTRIAL POLICY IN PERSPECTIVE

Before proceeding to examine some of the policies which have evolved to meet the needs of industry one important qualification should be made. It is simply that industrial policy *per se* cannot be considered in a vacuum. Monetary and fiscal variables, for example, and those macroeconomic policies designed to deal specifically with external trade and payments can have significant effects on the level of industrial activity. Similarly, the country's defence commitments and social policies with regard to housing in particular can affect the structure of industry and the level of output. It is worth emphasizing that such policies may or may not be consciously designed to promote the interests of industry. This applies also to certain measures which are, at first sight, narrowly industrial in scope.

Perhaps the best examples in this respect are regional and competition policies. The origins of the former can be traced back to the Special Areas legislation of the 1930s which offered limited financial inducements for firms to establish new plant capacity in certain designated areas of the country. As originally conceived the legislation was more the product of political embarrassment at the extent of human deprivation in the face of heavy localized unemployment. Whilst postwar regional policy has had the economic rationale of limiting inflationary pressure by attempting to secure the employment of underutilized capacity, social considerations and motives of political expediency have continued to loom large. The foundations of postwar competition policy were laid down in the Monopolies and Restrictive Practices Act of 1948. This measure was inspired by one of the most important documents on macroeconomic policy to have been published in Britain – the 1944 White Paper on employment policy which drew attention to the possibility that governmental attempts to stimulate aggregate demand might be frustrated by the pricing policies of large scale firms and collusive selling arrangements.

What this means is that it is extremely difficult to define the limits of industrial policy. Economic policies which affect industrial performance may well be the product of concern with 'non-industrial' issues and may even be inimical to the interests of industry. Conversely, some policies which appear to be overtly 'industrial' in application may derive much of their rationale from political and social considerations.

7.3 DELIBERATIVE INDUSTRIAL POLICIES

When we come to examine those measures which have been deliberately framed to improve the condition and performance of the industrial sector we are left with a twofold classification, one *supportive*, the other *innovative*. (See Clare Group, 1982, p. 12.) In the former category the most obvious example is the provision of financial aid for the reconstruction of specific industrial sectors or firms. Good illustrations of this approach are to be found in the Cotton Industry Act of 1959, passed by a Conservative government to help reduce surplus capacity in the domestic industry in the face of Far Eastern competition, and the offer in 1963 by the same administration of áid to the shipbuilding industry in the form of financial incentives for shipowners to place orders in British yards. The nationalization of Rolls Royce in 1971 as a result of financial failure due to the heavy cost of developing a new generation of jet engines and more recently, and most spectacular of all, the multi-million pound assistance to British Leyland (a firm nationalized in 1975 within the framework of the previous Conservative government's 1972 Industry Act) to enable the company to reconstruct its product range, have continued the established if *ad hoc* tradition of supportive intervention. As for innovative policies the main component has been the provision of information and finance in order to stimulate the introduction of new products and processes.

This approach to industrial policy has a surprisingly long history in Britain, going back to 1916 with the foundation of the state-sponsored Department of Scientific and Industrial Research, an organization which not only financed research directly in universities and colleges, but also encouraged industrialists to establish their own research associations. Similar functions were undertaken by the National Research Development Corporation (NRDC) which was established in 1948 to expedite the process of inventions where this was deemed to be in the national interest. Indeed, since 1945 more than 30 per cent of the funding for R and D in British industry has been derived from government sources, a percentage which comes near to the American commitment in this field and which outmatches considerably the performance of other OECD countries. In 1978 the British government spent 2.4 per cent of GDP to finance 47 per cent of the total cost of R and D. These figures again compare favourably with the USA, Japan and the rest of the EEC. It is noteworthy, however, that of this country's total expenditure of £3.5 billion more than half was devoted to defence projects. Only the US government spent a higher proportion of its R and D resources in this way and in the British case it was inevitably linked to a comparatively lower level of funding for civil projects than in the two most powerful EEC countries – France and Germany – and Japan. (See Prest and Coppock, 1982, pp. 237–8.)

Nevertheless, within the civil field, government expenditures under Department of Industry auspices for scientific and technological assistance rose in real terms in the three years after 1979. This was largely in response to the needs of the Product and Process Development Scheme (PPDS), launched in 1977 to encourage the introduction of 'new or significantly improved' products and processes and the Microprocessor Application Project (MAP) of 1978. The latter was the result of an appreciation of the importance of the new 'heartland' technology of the silicon chip where the speed of change both in relation to the technology itself and the pattern of markets was so rapid that it was decided that a deliberate effort was required of government to secure the widest possible dissemination of new knowledge and the application of microprocessors in industry. This was to be achieved by a combination of publicity, seminars, training programmes and the provision of finance for innovation.

In this context innovative policy with regard to small firms should be noted. This has its origins in the early 1970s following the deliberations of the Bolton Committee which drew attention to the competitive abilities of such firms (Bolton, 1971). The then Conservative government initiated a policy of financial reliefs, together with the establishment of official advisory services, an approach which has received greater attention more recently as a result of the 'Enterprise packages' which have been a feature of all Conservative budgets since 1979. The 1983 budget, for example, reduced the 'small companies' rate of corporation tax and raised the VAT registration threshold. Measures of this kind derive their rationale from the belief that small firms have a role to play in the regeneration of industry, both in terms of employment and the advance of technology, especially in micro-electronics. Indeed, invidious comparisons have been drawn between the British and West German economies in these respects with the latter displaying a much higher degree of structural diversity in terms of the relatively large number of small firms.[3] Although their numbers grew in Britain throughout the 1970s, the concentration of output remains heavily skewed in favour of large-scale enterprises. Thus it is a fair comment to point out that whilst there could well be 'ICIs and Unilevers of the future' within the ranks of today's small firms, policies to stimulate their foundation and expansion can only affect a relatively small proportion of industrial capacity (Prest and Coppock, 1982, p. 242).

'Deliberative' policies of the kind described above have thus been an important element in the search for improved industrial performance in both old and new sectors. It is true that the balance of financial support has been heavily in favour of the former, probably to the detriment of structural change in the economy as a whole, but from the standpoint of government the disparity in levels of assistance can be readily explained by the magnitude of the difficulties confronting such industries as shipbuilding, steel and vehicles. The experience of British Leyland, moreover, provides a good example of the opportunities presented by public subventions for desirable product and process innovations in established sectors.

7.4 THE CONCEPT OF INDUSTRIAL STRATEGY

(i) Background
One further component of industrial policy requires more extensive consideration since it provides a focal point for the discussion of some central issues concerning the limits of state intervention and its effectiveness. This is the concept of 'strategy' as enshrined in the National Plan of 1965 and the officially designated 'industrial strategy' launched under the auspices of the National Economic Development Council (NEDC) in 1975. The earlier venture was the product of a revulsion against the destabilizing effects on investment of the infamous 'stop-go' cycle and a growing awareness of Britain's relative economic decline. It was also heavily influenced by favourable perceptions of 'indicative planning' on the French model where the emphasis on a number of sectoral projects was designed to reduce the uncertainty inherent in investment decisions thereby creating a climate of expectations favourable to growth. It hardly needs to be said that the rationale and credibility of the National Plan were destroyed within a year of its publication as a result of the Labour government's deflationary measures of July 1966, which were intended to protect the existing exchange rate in the face of a deterioration in the external balance. This episode in British administrative and economic history is widely regarded as a fiasco of the worst order – a 'music-hall joke' which discredited the newly created Department of Economic Affairs and reconfirmed the status of the Treasury as the leading economic ministry (Opie, 1972). Yet it was only a decade later that a subsequent Labour administration resurrected the strategy concept, utilizing the NEDC (as opposed to a

separate department of state) as a vehicle for transforming Britain into 'a high-output, high wage economy. . . by improving our performance and productive potential' (Department of Industry, 1975). The original NEDC structure of tripartite committees was enhanced by the creation of sector working parties (SWPs) charged with the task of devising medium-term policies to raise productive potential and competitive standards in key growth sectors. The emphasis was on 'picking winners' and by 1980 forty SWPs had been formed, encompassing 40 per cent of total manufacturing output.

By the end of the Labour government's period of office in 1979 the SWPs had generated a considerable amount of activity, concentrating on recommendations for raising productivity levels, improving the quality of production by the provision of investment funds and manpower training, and extending the range of market opportunities by paying specific attention to selling techniques and the availability of export finance. The most ambitious initiatives to result from these deliberations were the funding of selected industry projects (including the Special Investment Scheme, SIS), and the financial support for MAP. Other noteworthy ventures were the Market Entry Guarantee Scheme (MEGS) which gave financial assistance in excess of £1 million in 1979 for the launching of seventeen new market-entry projects and the PPDS which supported ninety projects at a cost of nearly £8 million.

All of these measures were in accordance with the government's industrial strategy as set out in the White Paper of 1975. So too were the activities of the National Enterprise Board (NEB) which was formed in 1975 with £1000 million at its disposal to maintain productive employment, and to promote industrial efficiency and international competitiveness. Originally regarded with suspicion by some sections of political opinion as a possible vehicle for 'back-door' nationalization, the Board in practice devoted the greater part of its efforts to supervising the financial requirements of publicly-owned firms. By 1979 the bulk of its resources had been used for subventions to Rolls Royce and British Leyland in particular. This in turn produced criticisms that the Board was merely an institutional device for dealing with the problems of 'lame duck' firms but, as noted already, product and process innovation in established industries can be a worthy objective, all the more so in view of the catastrophic effect on regional and local unemployment if, say, British Leyland had been permitted to succumb to the pressure of market forces. It should also be borne in mind that by the end of the Labour government's period in office the NEB was committed to the support of the British computer and electronic office equipment industries and had allocated £50 million for the creation of Inmos, an entirely new microelectronics firm.

In reviewing recent trends in industrial policy it would be tempting to conclude that the Labour government's reinvocation of the strategy concept in 1975 marked a far more significant discontinuity in the history of state intervention than the ill-fated National Plan. This point is difficult to sustain. It has been noted that regional, competition and technology policies for industry have a long history in Britain but so too has the tripartite approach which came to the fore in the mid-1970s. Its evolution can be traced back to the official working parties established by the Board of Trade in the period 1945–6 which produced a large number of detailed reports on the postwar condition of British industry. It reappeared in the 1960s with the creation of the NEDC and its supporting economic development committees – the forerunners of the SWPs. It is also significant that several of the Labour government's specific measures, such as the support for British Leyland, the Accelerated Projects Scheme and the SIS were conceived within the framework of the previous Conservative administration's 1972 Industry Act. This legislation greatly extended the scope for government financial assistance in the aftermath of a brief and unsuccessful attempt at 'disengagement'.

So too with the Conservative government after 1979 it is, perhaps, all to easy to overemphasize the change in direction of industrial policy. Disengagement and privatization appeared to make striking headway with the formal abolition of the NEB (see below) and the sale of publicly owned assets, together with the reduction in scope of regional policies, the more rigorous approach to the granting of financial assistance under section 7 of the 1972 Industry Act and the refusal to intervene, despite significant political pressure, to prevent the closure of ailing plants in the manufacturing sector. These policies were no doubt inspired by the government's declared intention of 'rolling back the frontiers of the state' but their heterodoxy is arguably more apparent than real. The system of investment incentives inherited from the 1972 Act remained virtually intact and the counterparts of a lessening emphasis on regional policy *per se* were the Cabinet's decision in 1980 that the first manufacturing facility to be construted by Inmos should be located in South Wales, and the scale of the financial inducements offered to the Nissan company in an attempt to persuade the firm to establish a major vehicle assembly plant within the UK. Similarly, the creation of the British Technology Group by the merger of the NEB and the NRDC in 1981 did not lead to a reduction in the level of public funding for British Leyland or Rolls Royce. On the contrary, despite the government's objective of reducing direct financial support, the vehicle, aerospace, steel and shipbuilding industries received major subventions after 1979. These are not the only ways in which political rhetoric was inconsistent with reality: the selective assistance clauses of the 1972 Act remained in force and the inherited commitments to the PPDS and MAP were retained.

It is the 1979 Conservative government's retention of a fairly broad spectrum of established policy instruments that led the authors of a recent review of industrial policy to conclude that there was little that was 'consistent and explicit' in the government's actions and that 'the case for new initiatives must rest not on the notion of reversing a barely discernible trend towards disengagement and reliance on the market, but on a belief that long-established and broadly agreed British policies, are in some way inadequate or misdirected' (Clare Group, 1982, p. 4; see also NEDO, 1982). These remarks by the Clare Group of economists, emphasizing the basic continuity of industrial policy in the UK, preceded the general election of 1983 when the Conservative government was returned to office with an increased majority. A recommitment to privatization was soon announced and the decision to terminate the NEB-type functions of the British Technology Group could prove to be of more than symbolic importance if the government is able to time the sale of billions of pounds' worth of public sector assets in ways which avoid disrupting its own borrowing programme and which do not impinge on the available supply of capital to the extent that investment in private industry is jeopardized. Nevertheless, the views of the Clare Group are still of relevance, all the more so because they were advanced in the context of a debate between the advocates of some form of conscious industrial strategy and those who are intrinsically distrustful of centrist remedies for industrial weakness.

(ii) The case for an industrial strategy

The proponents of an industrial strategy place special emphasis on support programmes for technological innovation via R and D expenditures, and long-term restructuring of the industrial base by the more wholehearted provision of financial resources in the so-called 'sunrise' (mainly micro-electronics related) industries. This would require a reinvigorated commitment to tripartism with the possibility of borrowing from the 'planning' experiences of successful innovative countries, notably France and Japan. At a more detailed level, the historically narrow base of R and D expenditures in Britain – especially those sponsored by government – would have to be widened with extra resources being made available for, say, the PPDS, MEGS and the Research Requirements Boards. Secondly, some form of loan guarantee on Dutch lines for the subsidization of smaller innovative firms could be introduced, as well as measures to encourage financial institutions to lengthen the time horizon of their investments. Thirdly, UK industry as a whole should, whenever possible, apply 'best-practice' foreign technologies in order to maintain international competitiveness.

Fourthly, the formulation of policy itself could benefit from the creation of new institutions such as 'a separate industrial civil service, with its own recruitment and career structure, and regular interchanges of personnel with industry', and also an Industrial Structure Commission, with a similar organization to the defunct NEB and charged with the tasks of devising 'long-range strategies, both technological and marketing' in new industries and monitoring the performance of large-scale firms to provide early warning of commercial difficulties and hence limit the need for British Leyland-style rescue operations. Finally, virtually all 'strategists' are in favour of centrist policies to improve the overall quality of the British workforce, from management to the shop-floor, especially in terms of its awareness of and willingness to implement best-practice techniques. (See the papers by Pavitt, Stout and Jones in Carter (ed.), 1981.)

The common denominator underlying centrist opinion is a desire to emulate certain features of the Japanese, West German and French economies. Thus the advocacy of more broadly-based R and D expenditures is a reflection of the belief that British industrial performance since 1950 has been seriously constrained by excessive concentration on scientific and technological endeavours in aerospace and defence. Scarce and talented manpower has been siphoned off into these sectors and in view of the limited scale economies which have accrued in the light of American dominance of the relevant product markets, both finance and manpower would have been better employed in the more mundane sectors of machinery, vehicles and metal products – three of the areas where German and Japanese industry have had their most important market successes. Again, the advocacy of institutional reforms – indeed, the whole 'strategic' concept – is inspired by French and Japanese practice where the formulation of industrial policy is alleged to have benefited greatly from the interchange of personnel with shared backgrounds and experience between government and business, and also by these countries' ability, through national agencies, to back new strategic technologies according to broadly based and informed agreements on long-term national priorities.

The theoretical foundation of the centrist approach in so far as it pertains to industry's technological performance, is that reliance on market forces alone to stimulate innovation is misplaced in view of the fact that the private rate of return on an innovation, even when protected by patent, may well be far exceeded by the social benefit. This has been confirmed by impressive empirical evidence (see

Mansfield, 1980), and for these reasons alone it is argued that government promotion of R and D would be justified.

But in the British case there are two further factors to take into account – first, the present acute difficulties of much of the industrial sector and secondly the chronic nature of the country's economic decline in the light of the persistent inability of entrepreneurs to respond effectively to market signals. This is not to deny that intensified government intervention in the innovative process would lead to misallocations, but as one authority has pointed out, 'the fact that *some* public money will be wasted, on purposes for which private money might have been ventured and wasted instead, seems a poor reason for resigning oneself to the prospect of a slower rate of innovation – at a time when the process most especially needs to be speeded up' (Shonfield, 1981, p. 19; see also Stafford, 1981, p. 115). In short, to quote a former Economic Director of the National Economic Development Office,'Only the government can be relied upon to concern itself with the survival of a modern and relevant industrial base' (Stout, 1981, p. 123).

(iii) The anti-centrist case

In contradistinction to the centrist position other contributors to the debate, whilst acknowledging the current weakness of the British economy and its historic causes, have denied that a strategic approach to the problems of industry can have any significant impact on economic recovery. On the contrary, it is far more likely to undermine the prospects for revival in the industrial sector. It is possible to discern at least five strands in the anti-strategic stance: few of them are self-contained and together they constitute a powerful critique of more purposeful and assertive industrial policies (Clare Group, 1982, pp. 14–16, and Henderson, 1981).

Even at the most superficial level the telling point is made that, despite the basic continuity of deliberative policies and their tendency to become increasingly interventionist over time, the secular rate of unemployment has continued to rise since the mid-1950s. Will 'more of the same' reverse this apparently inexorable trend? Secondly, there is the central fact of a century-long process of relative decline, extraordinarily complex in its causes with economic, technical, political, social and cultural factors intermingled in varying degrees. Many commentators have offered diagnoses of 'the British sickness', notably Sir Henry Phelps Brown whose conclusion that a cure can only be effected by difficult and far-reaching changes in deeply embedded social, political and cultural institutions and practices merely serves to underline the lack of proportion between ends envisaged and centrist policy recommendations.

In a similar vein it is alleged that although some sections of centrist opinion display an awareness of the need to raise managerial standards in British industry, they underestimate the dimensions of the problem – the long-standing preference for pragmatism, historically weak provision for managerial and technical education and the legacy of complacency inherited from the days of imperial commerce. All of these factors have combined to produce 'a self-perpetuating state of inadequacy' of sufficient magnitude to render abortive an increase in the flow of R and D expenditures to promote greater competitiveness and productivity (Carter, 1981, p. 30).

Fourthly, the whole concept of an 'industrial strategy' has been attacked on the grounds that it neglects the principle of comparative advantage in international trade and ignores the problem of future uncertainty in a rapidly changing world. Thus, in view of Britain's peculiar factor endowment there may be positive advantages in belonging to the 'second division' of industrial countries, with less concentration on expensive and risky high-level technologies. Finally, it is claimed that much of centrist opinion is characterized by a dangerous belief in the country's 'manifest industrial destiny' – that it is right and proper that Britain should be constantly striving towards an industrial structure which reflects the current world technological frontier. As several commentators have observed, 'In so far as such attitudes prevail, a more assertive industrial strategy is likely to give ' rise to a succession of dubious or wasteful projects' (Clare Group, 1981, p. 15). The recent historical record is utilized to provide ample justification for such a view, with the civil nuclear power programme and the Concorde project as outstanding examples of a kind of 'bipartisan technological chauvinism' which seems to thrive in an overcentralized administrative structure whose hallmarks are secrecy and lack of personal accountability (Henderson, 1977, and Burn, 1978).

These anti-centrist strictures would appear at first sight to lend themselves to a *laissez-faire* approach to industrial policy. This is correct in three major respects. In the first instance considerable stress is placed upon the need for a long overdue review of the existing plethora of policy instruments, from investment incentives to export credit subsidies. This would enable policy-makers to concentrate on framing the kind of general and non-discriminatory measures which would enable them to establish some criteria of consistency in dealing with the inevitable assortment of 'lame ducks, high flyers, ewe lambs, sacred cows, dark horses and white elephants' (Henderson, 1981, pp. 176–7). At the same time the industrial structure as a whole would benefit from indirect measures such as revitalized competition policies, in order to break down established positions by encouraging the incentive to innovate.

If these are implicit criticisms of the trend of industrial policy since 1979, then this applies with even greater force to the third area of concern. As members of the Clare Group are well aware, their denigration of deliberative industrial policies inevitably highlights the importance of macroeconomic policy. It is unsurprising, therefore, that their conclusion that 'Supply responses are no substitute for demand management' goes hand in hand with a plea for more general measures to promote economic recovery as a whole, in particular, 'lower interest rates, a lower exchange rate and a less restrictive fiscal policy' (Clare Group, 1982, p. 16). Having said that there is *some* common ground with the centrists – the need to reduce the amount of defence-related R and D, to take account of (but not slavishly follow) foreign initiatives, and to raise managerial and technical standards, for example. Both sides of the debate also address themselves to the neglected area of 'adjustment policies', in other words government-sponsored measures to undermine the peculiarly British desire to achieve the fruits of economic growth while grimly maintaining outmoded attitudes and institutional structures which are inimical to innovation and structural change.

7.5 CONCLUSION

The greater part of this chapter has been devoted to the 'strategy' debate because this issue delineates the boundaries of orthodox opinion on the scope and effectiveness of industrial policy. In assessing the merits of the views advanced it should be stressed that there are strengths and weakness on both sides. The centrist position, for example, cannot simply be dismissed polemically as the product of national chauvinism in the guise of mercantilism. To argue that Britain should accept 'second division' status as an industrial power is to invite the retort that the perpetuation of the current low value-weight ratio of British manufactured exports would very quickly place the country in the zone of relegation, since there are many third-world competitors who can match British industry in the league of low-wage competition. As one advocate of an active supply-side policy has pointed out, Britain's relatively poor performance as an innovative country 'is not just a matter of national prestige, or of international standing'. It is in fact an issue with profound political and social implications: a higher standard of living as a result of accelerated industrial innovation could prove to be a powerful solvent of domestic tensions and encourage more tolerant attitudes towards the outside world (Pavitt, 1980, p. 2). It is difficult to regard these views as narrowly chauvinistic in the anti-centrist sense.

Secondly, to use the historical record of proven strategic and administrative errors in the investment/innovative process in order to downgrade the importance of deliberative policies is to luxuriate in a form of cynicism which assumes that there is no room for improvement in government policy and that decision-makers are incapable of learning from their mistakes. Although Britain has had more than its fair share of such errors, it is not inconceivable that anti-centrists are unduly pessimistic in this respect. Evidence to support this view is provided by the very public nuclear debate of the mid-1970s which culminated in the 1977 Windscale Inquiry on the reprocessing of nuclear waste. To quote from a major study of nuclear policy, 'This was not participatory government, whatever that might be, but it was in the end something approaching accountable government' (Williams, 1980, p. 317). In the nuclear field at least, therefore, this episode suggested that a 'learning process' had begun which could set precedents for future strategic decisions.

Turning to the anti-centrists there are two principal strengths in their approach. The first is the emphasis on the cumulative legacy of relative decline and the inevitable but necessary reminders that there are no easy solutions to Britain's economic predicament. To be fair to those in favour of some form of industrial strategy they too draw attention to the historical roots of the current malaise, but their disclaimers as to the possession of a monopoly of wisdom in the policy sphere are at times unconvincing. It would be wrong, moreover, to view the emphasis on macroeconomic objectives as the product of a myopic disregard of the importance of supply. It is simply a reflection of the uncontroversial belief that the impact of any conceivable combination of deliberative policies on improved industrial performance will be long delayed. In the meantime, therefore, according to anti-centrists in general and the Clare Group in particular, industrial expansion would receive a far greater stimulus from measures to promote general economic recovery. This is perhaps the most important lesson to be learnt from the debate on industrial strategy – that macro- and microeconomic policies are not substitutes: they are mutually dependent and policy-makers ignore this central fact at their peril.

NOTES

1   See, for example, Caves and Associates (1968), Swords-Isherwood (1980), Taylor (1978), Phelps Brown (1977), Wiener (1981) and Pollard (1982).

2   The literature in this area includes the following useful studies: Kaldor (1980), Freeman (1978), Young and Lowe (1974), NRDC (1978), EEC (1979) and NEDO (1980).
3   See Ray (1978), pp. 75–6. See also Rothwell and Zegveld (1981) and Bollard (1983).

REFERENCES

Beckerman, W. (ed.) (1972) *The Labour Government's Economic Record: 1964–1970* (London: Duckworth).

Blackaby, F. (ed.) (1978) *De-industrialisation* (London: Heinemann).

Bollard, A. (1983) 'Technology, Economic Change and Small Firms', *Lloyds Bank Review*, January, pp. 42–56.

Bolton, (1971) *Report of the Committee of Inquiry on Small Firms*, Cmnd 4811 (London: HMSO).

Burn, D. (1978) *Nuclear Power and the Energy Crisis: Politics and the Atomic Industry*, Trade Policy Research Centre (London: Macmillan).

Carter, C. (1981) 'Reasons for not Innovating', in C. Carter (ed.) (1981).

Carter, C. (ed.) (1981) *Industrial Policy and Innovation* (London: Heinemann).

Caves, R. E. and Associates (1968) *Britain's Economic Prospects*, Brookings Institution (London: Allen & Unwin).

Clare Group (1982) 'Problems of Industrial Recovery', *Midland Bank Review*, Spring, pp. 9–16.

Cook, C. and Ramsden, J. (eds.) (1978) *Trends in British Politics since 1945* (London: Macmillan).

Department of Industry (1975) *An Approach to Industrial Strategy*, Cmnd. 6315 (London: HMSO).

EEC (Commission of the European Communities) (1979) *Changes in Industrial Structure in the European Economies since the Oil Crisis, 1973–1978*, Brussels.

Freeman, C. F. (1978) 'Technical Innovation and British Trade Performance', in F. Blackaby (ed.) (1978).

Henderson, P. D. (1977) 'Two British Errors: Their Probable Size and Some Possible Lessons', *Oxford Economic Papers*, vol. 29, pp. 186–94.

Henderson, P. D. (1981) 'Comment', in C. Carter (ed.) (1981).

Kaldor, M. (1980) 'Technical Change in the Defence Industry', in K. Pavitt (ed.) (1980).

Kirby, M. W. (1981) *The Decline of British Economic Power since 1870* (London: Allen & Unwin).

Mansfield, E. (1980) 'Measuring the Social and Private Rates of Return on Innovation', in *Economic Effects of Space and other Advanced Technologies* (Strasbourg: Council of Europe).

NEDO (National Economic Development Office) (1980) *British Industrial Performance* (London: NEDO).

NEDO (National Economic Development Office) (1982) *Industrial Policy in the UK: Memorandum by the Director General* (London: NEDO).

NRDC (National Research Development Corporation) (1978) 'Evidence to the [Wilson] Committee to Review the Functioning of Financial Institutions' (London: HMSO).

Opie, R (1972) 'Economic Planning and Growth' in W. Beckerman (ed.) (1972).

Pavitt, K. (ed.) (1980) *Technical Innovation and British Economic Performance* (London: Macmillan).

Phelps Brown, Sir H. (1977) 'What is the British Predicament?', *The Three Banks Review*, December, pp. 3–29.

Pollard, S. (1982) *The Wasting of the British Economy: British Economic Policy 1945 to the Present* (London: Croom Helm).

Prest, A. R. and Coppock, D. J. (1982) *The UK Economy: a Manual of Applied Economics* (London: Weidenfeld and Nicolson).

Ray, G. F. (1978) 'Comment', in F. Blackaby (ed.) (1978).

Rothwell, R. and Zegveld, W. (1981) *Industrial Innovation and Public Policy: Preparing for the 1980s and the 1990s* (London: Frances Pinter).

Shonfield, A. (1981) 'Innovation: Does Government have a Role?' in C. Carter (ed.) (1981).

Stafford, G. B. (1981) *The End of Economic Growth? Growth and Decline in the UK since 1945* (Oxford: Martin Robertson).

Stout, D. K. (1981) 'The Case for Government Support of R & D and Innovation', in C. Carter (ed.) (1981).

Swords-Isherwood, N. (1980) 'British Management Compared', in K. Pavitt (ed.) (1980).

Taylor, R. (1978) 'Scapegoats for National Decline: the Trade Unions since 1945', in C. Cook and J Ramsden (eds) (1978).

Walker, W. B. (1980) 'Britain's Industrial Performance 1850–1950: A Failure to Adjust', in K Pavitt (ed.) (1980).

Wiener, M. (1981) *English Culture and the Decline of the Industrial Spirit* (Cambridge: CUP).

Williams, R. (1980) *The Nuclear Power Decisions* (London: Croom Helm).

Young, S. and Lowe, A. V. (1974) *Intervention in the Mixed Economy: the Evolution of British Industrial Policy 1964–1972* (London: Croom Helm).

QUESTIONS FOR DISCUSSION

1 What, in your view, are the principal causes of weak industrial performance in the UK?

2 How do you account for the relatively high level of government-sponsored R and D expenditures in the UK since 1945?

3 Did the advent of the Conservative government in 1979 mark a significant discontinuity in industrial policy?

4 Critically assess the view that the regeneration of British industry

necessitates an active and purposeful policy of strategic intervention by the state.
5   Discuss the contention that 'supply responses are no substitute for demand management'.
6   To what extent can government promotion of small firms contribute to the regeneration of the British industrial economy?

8 The Amount of Labour Supplied and Labour Supply

C. V. BROWN

In this chapter I want to discuss both the amount of labour supplied and labour supply. The amount of labour supplied refers to the amount of work actually done and labour supply refers to the amount of work people would like to do at current wage rates. Unemployment is one measure of the difference between the amount of work people would like to do and the amount of work they actually do, as discussed more fully in Chapter 3.

8.1 LABOUR SUPPLIED

An obvious determinant of the amount of work done is the total population. Figure 8.1 shows actual and projected population for the UK (that is, Great Britain and Northern Ireland) from 1951 to 1981. It can be seen that the population rose from about 50 million in 1951 to about 56 million in 1981. It is officially projected that the population will rise to 58 million by 1996.

It is clear, however, that not all members of the population are available for work. Babies and the very elderly clearly cannot work but just which age groups should be counted as available for work will depend on social conventions, and on the laws affecting the ages of full-time education and retirement, to take only two obvious examples. In Britain the compulsory minimum school-leaving age has been raised since the war from fourteen to sixteen in two stages and in addition a higher proportion of young people have chosen to continue their education beyond the minimum age legally acceptable for leaving school. There are also rules and conventions about retirement. One of the ways in which men and women are treated differently in Britain is that the official retirement age for women is sixty while it is sixty-five for men – a strange form of discrimination because women have a higher life expectancy than men.

It is useful to define the population between the ages when people are legally supposed to be at school and the official retirement age as *the population of working age*. It is, of course, true that some people

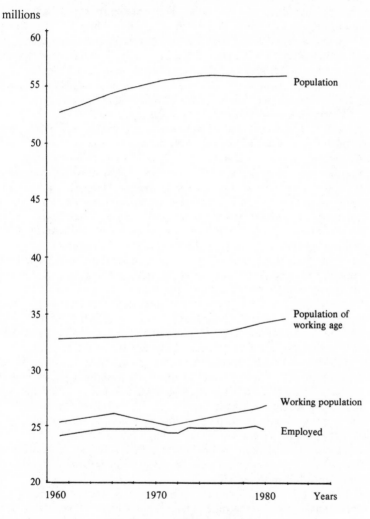

millions

Figure 8.1   UK population

SOURCE: Annual Abstract of Statistics, various, Table 6.1.

already work while still at school and some carry on working beyond the official age of retirement. It is also true that many people who are of working age are not available for work. There are many reasons for this, ranging from being in prison to having very severe physical or mental handicaps, but one reason is of special interest. Some perople prefer not to work and have a means of support which makes it possible for them not to work. The most important such group numerically is undoubtedly married women. Until fairly recently there was a convention in some social groups against women working after they were married and particularly after they had children, but this convention is very rapidly disappearing amongst younger people. Other groups voluntarily not working include students and small numbers with independent means or state support.

If we subtract from the *population of working age* those not wishing to work we are left with *the working population. The working population* may be defined as people of working age who *wish* to work *at current wage rates*. I have stressed *wish* to work for two reasons, first because as we have seen, not every person of working age will wish to work, and second because some people who would like to have jobs are unable to get a job. I also stressed at *current wage rates* because some might be willing to work only at much higher wage rates. For example, a mother with a young child might be able to earn a low wage (perhaps because of having little training) and not want to' work because of the need to care for her child. If the wage were high enough so she could pay for better domestic appliances and send her child to a nursery shcool, she might wish to work.

Figure 8.1 shows the total population, the population of working age and the working population for selected years in the period 1951–81. The least accurate of these figures is the working population. The reason that it is less accurate than the others is that it is the sum of the employed population (people who actually work) and the unemployed population. The unemployed are in principle those who are not at work who would like to work at current wages but in practice they are those who are registered as unemployed. It seems likely therefore that the working population is actually higher than the figure shows, and that the margin of error will have increased as unemployment has increased. The chapters by Paul Hare in Part I and Michael Jackson in Part II of this volume consider the nature and causes of unemployment in rather more detail.

Figure 8.1 which includes both men and women conceals an important difference that has emerged between the sexes. It can be seen from Figure 8.2 that the population of working age has grown at similar rates for both sexes. The working population of men, however, has fallen from nearly 17 million in 1966 to just over 16 million in

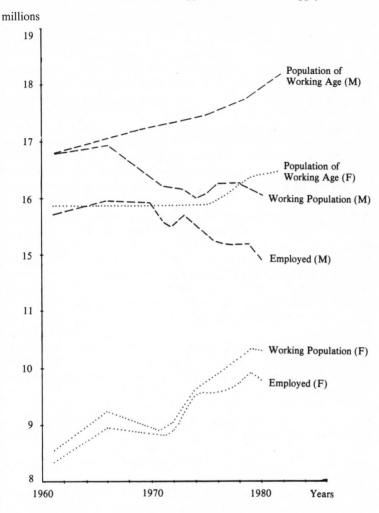

Figure 8.2   Working population in the UK

SOURCE: Annual Abstract of Statistics, various.

1980. During the same period the female working population has increased from 9.2 million to 10.3 million. Thus while the total working population changed very little, nearly a million men left the labour force and were replaced by over a million women. This will partly reflect changing opportunities for women to work in light industries and in service industries and in part it will reflect the changing social attitudes towards work mentioned earlier.

As already noted, the working population includes both the employed and the unemployed. Figure 8.2 also shows employment and unemployment by sex. It can be seen that the fall in male employment has been even greater than the fall in the male work force with the difference, of course, being unemployment. Female employment has risen but less rapidly than the female work force, again reflecting the growth in unemployment.

The total amount of work done depends on the number of workers but also on the quantity and quality of work done by each worker. The quality of work is unfortunately virtually impossible to measure across a whole population, but we can look at weeks, days and hours of work. Weeks of work have been falling because of increasing entitlement to paid holidays. In 1961 97 per cent of manual workers were entitled to only two weeks' paid holiday. By the end of 1981 80 per cent were entitled to holidays of four weeks or more. A lot of work is lost because of sickness and invalidity. In 1979/80 females lost 83 million days through sickness and males 276 million days and these levels represented substantial increases over the comparable figures five years earlier. Widely varying amounts of time are lost through industrial disputes. In some years as little as 5 million days (as in 1976) are lost, while in 1979 nearly 30 million days were lost. Days lost through stoppages are far less than days lost through illness, but stoppages receive far more attention in the press, perhaps justifiably for they will often cause greater disruption.

The final measure of the quantity of work being done that I want to mention is hours of work. Average weekly hours worked by males in manufacturing have fallen from just over 46 in 1967 to 44 in 1979 and the figures for full time females have fallen from 38.0 to 37.2 over the same period.

To sum up it seems reasonable to infer that total hours worked have fallen by more than the fall in employment shown in Figure 8.2. The reasons for this are longer holidays, more time off sick, shorter hours at work during the weeks worked, and the switch from male to female employment (given that males work longer than full time women *and* that more women work part time).

8.2 LABOUR SUPPLY

Thus far I have concentrated on the amount of work done, and I now want to turn to a discussion of the amount of work people would like to do. Most people would prefer to do some work to doing none. There may be several reasons for this, such as the social conventions favouring work, enjoyment of the work, and enjoyment of social interaction at work. Economists, however, concentrate particularly on the point that if people go to work they will earn money that will enable them to purchase goods and services they would not be able to purchase if they were not at work. In other words, people attach more weight, or to use economists' jargon more utility, to the goods and services they can buy with the extra income, than they attach to the leisure they have to forego to earn that income. Given a free choice, people will wish to work up to the point where the extra utility from an extra unit of income just balances the loss of utility from the associated loss of leisure. Now it seems reasonable to imagine that the amount that people will want to work will depend on how much extra goods and services they will be able to buy if they give up an hour of their leisure. In an economy without taxes the amount of goods and services one can buy depends on the level of consumer prices and on the wage rate, which for convenience we can assume to be an hourly wage rate. An important question is how a change in the wage rate will affect the amount of work a person would wish to do. Suppose we consider the case of a person who is able to work any number of hours he wishes to work and who is paid £2 an hour and chooses to work forty hours in the week. How would this person react to a drastic cut in his wage to £1 an hour? Would he now wish to work more than forty hours or less than forty hours? There are, in fact, likely to be two forces at work, one making him wish to work more, the other making him wish to work less.

Let us look at what would happen if the person continued to work forty hours. His total weekly pay would fall from £80 (£2 x 40 hours) to £40 (£1 x 40 hours). This drop in his income would mean he could now purchase fewer goods and services. His real income has thus fallen and it seems reasonable to imagine that the effect of this fall in real income will be to make the person wish to work longer to minimize the fall in his living standards. Economists call this the *income effect*. With a fall in the wage rate the income effect will normally cause people to work more and, conversely, if the wage rate went up, the income effect would normally cause people to work less. However, there is another effect. When the wage rate was £2 an hour, people were able to gain £2 worth of goods and services by giving up an hour of their leisure. If the wage is only £1 the reward for giving up an hour of leisure is reduced. This means that leisure is now relatively cheaper so people will want more leisure instead of extra income. Economists call this the *substitution effect*. When the wage falls, people will wish to substitute leisure for income, that is they will wish

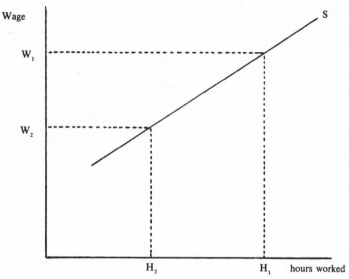

Figure 8.3   Positively sloped labour supply

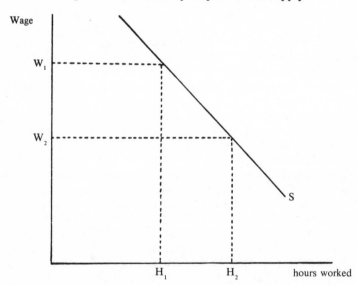

Figure 8.4   Negatively sloped labour supply

In Figure 8.3 a cut in the wage rate reduces desired hours of work because the substitution effect is stronger than the income effect. In Figure 8.4 a cut in the wage rate increases work because the income effect is stronger than the substitution effect.

to work less. Conversely, if the wage rate rose, the substitution effect would cause people to want to work more. To summarize, if the wage rate falls, the income effect will normally lead to more work and the substitution effect to less work. Because the income effect and substitution effect work in opposite directions it is impossible to know *a priori* whether a fall in the wage will lead to more work or less work. Figures 8.3 and 8.4 illustrate the two possibilities.

Special interest is sometimes focussed on changes in wage rates brought about by the tax system. In the example in the preceding paragraphs a tax of 50 per cent on all income would have the effect of reducing a gross wage of £2 an hour to a net wage of £1 an hour. So tax changes, like changes in wage rates, can cause people to work either more or less, since it is the net wage (that is, after tax) which is relevant to people's income–leisure choices.

One of the major research interests of the Economics Department at Stirling University has been to investigate the relationship between wages after tax, and labour supply. We are currently engaged in a project for HM Treasury looking at exactly this question. Not only is the effect of taxation on work incentives an important topic in its own right but it is also an interesting example of the kind of problem one can encounter when applying economic analysis to real-life problems. In this case there are numerous technical difficulties to overcome because the real world is much more complicated than the example above. In practice people may not be allowed to choose their hours of work (because many jobs specify the hours required) and there are a variety of different wage rates, for example, for overtime and for second jobs, and in reality not all income is taxed at the same rate, most importantly because people receive allowances which mean that the first part of their income is tax free. It turns out that investigating these features of the real world is both very important and very difficult.

While it would not be appropriate to discuss these difficulties in detail here, I hope I have made it clear that it would be wrong to assume that cuts in income tax will necessarily lead to people wanting to work longer.

This account has deliberately neglected an important determinant of the amount of labour actually supplied. The important element is, of course, the demand for labour. The amount of work actually done will depend on both labour supply and labour demand. However, there is no need to pursue this topic here, since it was already covered in Chapter 2.

8.3 THE FUTURE

What of the future? It would be easy to omit any discussion of the future as too uncertain, but it may be worth a little speculation. Demography provides a few clues. Every year young people enter the labour force and older people reach retirement age. The post-war baby boom which peaked in the mid-sixties means that we are now at the peak for people of school-leaving age, as can be seen from Table 8.1. If we subtract the number of people reaching retirement age from the number of people of school-leaving age, we will have a first approximation to the change in population of working age (further approximations would examine net migration and death rates). The table shows this peaking at 340,000 in 1981 and falling to less than half that number a decade later. This suggests that the population of working age will grow more slowly. If trends towards longer holidays, earlier retirement, more time off for sickness and shorter hours all continue, the total quantity of work, measured in hours, could well fall. If that happens, then higher incomes can only come about through the production of more goods *and services* per hour. Also, fewer jobs will need to be created to maintain full employment than would be the case if either the population of working age continued to rise at its present rate, or weeks, days and hours of work did not fall.

Table 8.1   Changes in population of working age

Year	UK population (000s) Age 16		Age 60 Age 65		Approximate changes in population of working age (a)+(b)−(c)−(d)
	M	F	F	M	
	(a)	(b)	(c)	(d)	
1961	397	381	323	203	+ 252
1966	387	370	351	258	+ 159
1971	388	373	348	261	+ 152
1976	441	422	317	270	+ 276
1981	493	471	376	248	+ 340
1986	442	417	314	295	+ 250
1991	358	338	299	257	+ 140
1995	360	339	283	246	+ 170

SOURCE: Office of Population Censuses and Surveys. Population Projections, 1970–2010, 1978-2018.

Many people are of course concerned about the effects of technological change on employment. Technological change will simultaneously both eliminate some traditional jobs and create new ones, so a critical question concerns the balance between the two. While I have no crystal ball I happen to be a qualified optimist on this topic and conclude this chapter by explaining why that is the case.

I am an optimist partly because history has frequently falsified prophecies that the latest invention would create mass unemployment and partly because it should be possible to increase both aggregate demand and aggregate supply for the foreseeable future. The world will of course run short of particular resources. For example, in your lifetime the world supply of oil may well shrink sharply, making it necessary both to conserve energy and to look for substitutes. These and other shortages will almost certainly mean changes in techniques and in the composition of output. In this context it is fortunate that as real incomes increase people choose to consume a decreasing proportion of goods and an increasing proportion of services (services not only require fewer resources but also tend to be more labour-intensive).

My optimism is qualified because the pace of technological change is very high and such rapid technological change requires a high rate of change in human response and people may be unwilling to change at the required pace. It is easy to understand a worker resisting change if his or her own job is threatened, but if the best techniques are not adopted in, say, this country, then people throughout the world will be inclined to buy goods where the value for money is best.

What if my basic optimism is unfounded and despite everyone's best efforts jobs were destroyed faster than others were created. Would this necessarily be a disaster? The circumstances we are imagining are ones where repetitive industrial and clerical jobs disappear faster than new ones are created. This situation would not necessarily be a disaster, but it would require substantial reorganization. In these circumstances we would actually be able to produce a lot of goods without the associated drudgery. In many ways, this would be a good thing, but what society would have to face up to is finding fair ways of distributing what is produced. It would also need to find ways for people to occupy themselves meaningfully.

FURTHER READING

Brown, C. V. (1983) *Taxation and the Incentive to Work*, 2nd ed., Oxford University Press.

Laidler, D. (1981) *Introduction to Microeconomics*, 2nd ed., Phillip Allen.

HM Treasury (1982) 'Alleviating Unemployment', Economic Progress Report No. 148, August.

HM Treasury (1982) 'Recent Trends in Labour Productivity', Economic Progress Report No. 141, January.

See also suggestions in Chapter 2.

QUESTIONS FOR DISCUSSION

1   What has happened to the amount of labour supplied in Britain since the mid-1960s?
2   Can you use income and substitution effects to account for the fact that the working week is a lot shorter now than it was in the mid-nineteenth century?
3   What effect will technological advances such as the silicon chip have on the job prospects of people now at school?

9 Job Creation and Related Programmes

MICHAEL JACKSON

9.1 RECENT TRENDS IN UNEMPLOYMENT: THE BACKGROUND TO JOB CREATION

In the thirty years following the Second World War Britain enjoyed relatively low rates of unemployment. The rate varied and on occasions rose fairly sharply but such rises were reversed within a year or two. Table 9.1 shows that from 1975 onwards the position

Table 9.1   Unemployment rate, UK, 1960–82

Year	Unemployment rate*	Year	Unemployment rate*
1960	1.7	1971	3.5
1961	1.6	1972	3.8
1962	2.1	1973	2.7
1963	1.7	1974	2.7
1964	1.5	1975	4.1
1965	1.6	1976	5.7
1966	2.5	1977	6.2
1967	2.5	1978	6.1
1968	2.5	1979	5.7
1969	2.5	1980	7.4
1970	2.6	1981	11.4
		1982	13.8

* Numbers show registered unemployed as a percentage of estimated total number of employees

SOURCES: Annual Abstract of Statistics, 1972, p. 143; 1982, p. 163; Employment Gazette, November 1982, p. 518.

changed significantly. Between 1974 and 1975 the unemployment rate rose from 2.7 per cent to 4.1 per cent: more importantly, though, this rise was not reversed in subsequent years. Unemployment rates declined in 1978 and 1979 but only marginally and the upward trend began again in 1980, so that by 1982 almost 14 per cent of the workforce (over 3 million people) was unemployed, about five times what the rate had been in 1974.

Table 9.2   Unemployment by duration, Great Britain, 1974–82

Year	2 weeks or less	2–4 weeks	4–8 weeks	8–13 weeks	13–26 weeks	26–52 weeks	Over 52 weeks
1974	20.8	12.1	11.3	10.3	14.3	10.9	20.2
1975	15.3	15.4	14.4	11.8	16.1	12.3	14.7
1976	9.8	7.4	12.4	12.3	20.3	20.9	17.1
1977	9.5	7.2	11.4	11.4	18.7	19.7	22.2
1978	7.9	6.9	10.3	10.2	17.8	19.9	27.0
1979	6.2	6.2	10.2	10.6	17.8	18.8	30.2
1980	8.6	7.1	12.0	12.0	18.7	18.3	23.3
1981	6.2	5.4	9.9	11.4	22.1	24.6	20.4
1982	4.3	4.6	8.0	8.7	17.4	23.9	33.1

Notes: (1) Figures in the table are percentages of the total number of people unemployed at that time. (2) Figures for 1980-82 cover the UK (i.e. Great Britain and Northern Ireland).

SOURCES: Department of Employment Gazette 1977, October, p. 1159; Gazette 1980, October, p. 533; Employment Gazette 1982, October, p. 534.

Alongside this rise in unemployment rates, another important trend might be noted. Over the same period the average duration of unemployment increased. Table 9.2 shows that whereas in 1974 only 31 per cent of those unemployed had been out of work for six months or more, in 1982 the comparable proportion was 57 per cent. Many people argue that long-term unemployment is a particularly important problem, causing severe social as well as economic difficulties.

Of course, Britain has not been alone in experiencing a rise in the level of unemployment since the mid-1970s. Most Western nations

Table 9.3   Standardized unemployment rates – international comparisons, 1970–82

Per cent of total labour force

	1970	1971	1972	1973	1974	1975	1976	1977	1978	1979	1980	1981	1982
Australia	1.6	1.9	2.6	2.3	2.6	4.8	4.7	5.6	6.2*	6.2*	6.0	5.7	7.1
Austria	1.4	1.3	1.2	1.1	1.4	1.7	1.8	1.6	2.1	2.1	1.9	2.5	3.5
Belgium	2.1	2.2	2.7	2.8	3.1	5.1	6.6	7.5	8.1	8.4	9.0	11.1	13.0*
Canada	5.6	6.1	6.2	5.5	5.3	6.9	7.1	8.0	8.3	7.4	7.5	7.5	9.5
Finland	5.6	6.1	6.2	5.5	5.3	6.9	7.1	8.0	8.3	7.4	7.5	7.5	10.9
France	2.4	2.6	2.7	2.6	2.8	4.1	4.4	4.7	5.2	5.9	6.3	7.3	8.0*
Germany	0.8*	0.9*	0.8*	0.8*	1.6*	3.6*	3.7*	3.6*	3.5*	3.2*	3.0*	4.4*	6.1*
Italy	5.3	5.3	6.3	6.2	5.3	5.8	6.6	7.0	7.1	7.5	7.4	8.3	8.9
Japan	1.1	1.2	1.4	1.3	1.4	1.9	2.0	2.0	2.2	2.1	2.0	2.2	2.4
Netherlands	1.0*	1.3*	2.2*	2.2*	2.7*	3.9*	4.2*	4.1	4.1	4.1	4.7	7.0	9.6*
Norway	1.6*	1.5*	1.7	1.5	1.5	2.3	1.8	1.5	1.8	2.0	1.7	2.0	2.6
Spain	2.4*	3.1*	3.1*	2.5*	2.6*	3.7*	4.7*	5.2*	6.9*	8.5	11.2	14.0	15.9
Sweden	1.5	2.5	2.7	2.5	2.0	1.6	1.6	1.8	2.2	2.1	2.0	2.5	3.1
United States	4.8	5.8	5.5	4.8	5.5	8.3	7.5	6.9	5.9	5.7	7.0	7.5	9.5

Note to Table 9.3: Data have been adjusted (as far as possible) both to preserve comparability over time and to conform with the definitions drawn up by the International Labour Organisation. The adjustments mainly affect countries that base their unemployment statistics on registration records maintained by employment offices. Where necessary the OECD has tried to adjust 'registered' unemployment with a view to including unemployed persons not covered on the register and to excluding employed persons still carried on the register. For several countries the adjustment procedure used is similar to that of the US Department of Labor. Minor differences may appear mainly because the rates published by the US Department of Labor refer to the civilian labour force. Series adjusted by the OECD are marked by an asterisk (*).

SOURCE: OECD Economic Outlook, July 1983, No. 33, p. 169.

have faced similar problems. Table 9.3 shows that the rise in unemployment rates in Britain has been matched fairly closely in a number of other countries (the best example is Belgium), and that even those countries that have not suffered as much as Britain have not escaped entirely (unemployment rates in Japan, for example, are still very low by comparison though they have also risen significantly since 1974).

Of course, the rise in the level of unemployment has not affected all sections of society equally: some groups have suffered much more than others. A great deal of attention has centred on youth unemployment, for in most countries young people have suffered more from unemployment than older workers and unemployment has risen faster amongst such groups. Table 9.4 shows the unemployment rate for young people under 18, and 18–19 years old between 1965 and 1982. If the figures in this table are compared with those given in Table 9.1 then it can be seen that unemployment amongst young people, especially those under 18, rose much faster than amongst other sections of the community in the mid-1970s: between 1976 and 1978, for example, the overall unemployment rate rose from 5.7 per cent to 6.1 per cent, but amongst young people under 18 the rate rose from 8.5 per cent to 14.5 per cent. It appears that young people are affected more quickly by a downturn in economic activity than the rest of the population; the reason for this is that many of them are school-leavers entering the labour market for the first time, and as a result are particularly vulnerable to cutbacks in recruitment by employers.

Other groups that have also suffered particularly badly during

Table 9.4   Youth unemployment, Great Britain, 1965–82

	% Under 18	% 18–19
1965	1.5	1.6
1966	1.3	1.5
1967	2.3	2.9
1968	2.3	3.2
1969	2.1	3.0
1970	2.5	3.4
1971	3.2	4.3
1972	5.4	6.8
1976	8.5	9.5
1977	13.5	10.3
1978	14.5	10.9
1979	11.8	10.4
1980	11.0	10.5
1981	19.2	17.2
1982	22.6	22.9

Notes: 1 All percentage rates are estimates. The rates between 1965 and 1972 are based on the total number of employees in the relevant age group and the number registered as unemployed. The basis of the calculation for the rate from 1976 is given in the Employment Gazette, July 1977, pp. 718–19. Rates for 1973–5 were not published. 2 All rates refer to January of the year concerned. Rates fluctuate considerably throughout the year and on occasion have been very much higher in July than in January because of the number of school leavers unable to find employment.

SOURCE: (a) Up to 1972: Annual Abstract of Statistics, relevant years; British Labour Statistics, relevant years. (b) 1976 and after: Employment Gazette, December 1979, p. 1258; Employment Gazette, October 1982, p. 537.

periods of high unemployment have included racial minorities. Not all racial minorities have suffered worse than average: in Britain, the groups which have suffered particularly badly have been West Indian and Pakistani/Bangladeshi males from abroad, while some other non-white groups from abroad, like Chinese, have had a marginally lower unemployment rate than the average for white males born in the UK. Further analysis of the unemployment figures would enable other groups who suffer worse than average to be identified. These groups include workers with handicaps or a history of illness, older workers and employees in certain occupations.

9.2 THE ROLE OF JOB CREATION

Most Western governments have introduced a variety of different special employment measures in recent years as one of the ways of responding to rising unemployment. In many cases the measures have been targetted on some of the groups identified above as having been particularly badly affected by the rise in unemployment; amongst these the young are undoubtedly the best example.

The special employment measures introduced in this context have included a number of different types of job subsidy, devices to reduce the size of the active labour force (like early retirement and further educational provision), in some cases the expansion or introduction of special training facilities, and job creation schemes. The balance between these measures has differed from one country to another, yet in most cases job creation schemes have played an important role.

Job creation measures have a long history. For example, they were used during the inter-war period with public works programmes. However, there is little doubt that the bulk of the job creation measures introduced recently differ substantially from such endeavours: they have been much more sophisticated attempts by governments to increase the level of employment with considerable attention being paid not only to the amount of employment created but also to the quality of the work provided and the effect that the experience of doing the work will have on the person doing it.

The real forerunner of the recent job creation measures is the range of provision introduced in the USA in the 1960s. Under the Manpower Development and Training Act and the Economic Opportunity Act, a number of programmes were introduced to give better work opportunities to groups finding it difficult to obtain steady employment. The programmes included the Neighbourhood Youth Corps (which helped 16–21 year olds from poor families), Operation Mainstream (designed to help older workers find employment), New Careers (aimed more specifically at professional careers) and Job Opportunities in the Business Sector (which concentrated on helping private industry to employ hard-core unemployed and disadvantaged workers). These programmes were linked to the 'War on Poverty', which began to be phased out in the late 1960s and early 1970s.

Nevertheless, some of them survived beyond this period, in a modified form, and they have been seen as an interesting development in their own right.

In some ways, however, the Canadian Local Initiative Programme has had a more direct influence than the USA programmes of the 1960s on schemes in other countries. The Canadian Programme was introduced in 1971 and had two aims: one was to provide work for the unemployed, while the other was to provide a service to the community. These dual aims were mirrored in many subsequent developments in other Western nations.

In Britain, interest began to be shown in the current generation of job-creation programmes in the early 1970s. The first specific programme, Community Industry, was started in 1971. However, Community Industry was targetted on disadvantaged young people who would have had difficulty obtaining employment, no matter what the market, and therefore it might be claimed that it was not simply a straightforward job-creation programme. No such caveats are needed for the two programmes introduced in 1975 and 1976, Job Creation and Work Experience, and as a result they are often referred to as the first of the current generation of job-creation programmes in Britain.

The Job Creation Programme lasted for three years, from 1975 to 1978. In this period, it provided places for about 120,000 people mainly, though not entirely, in the age-group 16–24. The explicit aims of the programme were to undertake tasks which would have some community benefit (either by improving the local environment or by assisting in the solution of social or community problems) and to provide work which would benefit participants (if possible through training, though it was stressed that Job Creation was not meant to be a training programme as such). The bulk of the projects were provided by public authorities, though a substantial number (around a third) were provided by voluntary or charitable organizations. A large proportion of projects were based on construction and environmental improvement (over 40 per cent) and education, social service and research work (over 40 per cent): few projects were based on production/manufacturing.

The Work Experience Programme was started a year later than Job Creation though it terminated at the same time. In many ways it was a similar type of programme, providing work essentially for young people. However, the targetting was much tighter, specifying that only 16–18 year olds were to be eligible for places, and the orientation of the programme was different, placing considerably more emphasis on giving participants an experience which would enhance their job skills and as a result their chances of gaining employment subsequently. One corollary of this orientation was that much less emphasis was placed on 'getting the job done', or on the 'community benefit' of the work than in job creation. In practice, there was also another major difference between the Job Creation and Work Experience Programmes in that the latter involved private enterprise much more than the former: about 80 per cent of all places on the Work Experience Programme were provided by private industry, whereas the comparable figure for the Job Creation Programme was about 5 per cent. A substantial proportion of projects (about a quarter) were based on manufacturing and a similar proportion were based on the distributive trades, with most of the balance being accounted for by other service activity. The Work Experience Programme provided places for about 40,000 people in total.

The Job Creation and Work Experience Programmes were both terminated in 1978 but the idea of job creation, as such, was not abandoned. Instead, two new programmes were introduced, the Youth Opportunities Programme and the Special Temporary Employment Programme. The Youth Opportunities Programme, designed for the 16–18 age group, contained two different kinds of provision. One was a range of courses designed to prepare young people for work: three types of courses were offered – assessment or short induction courses, short industrial courses, and remedial or preparatory courses. The other was the provision of different kinds of work experience: four were offered – work experience on employers' premises, project-based work experience, training workshops and community service. In practice work experience has been by far the most important type of provision (according to the numbers covered), providing about four-fifths of all places, and the overwhelming majority of work experience places were offered on employers' premises.

The Special Temporary Employment Programme was designed for a different age group (those aged 19–25, and those over 25 who had been unemployed for more than a year), and was aimed at those living in the areas worst affected by the recession. The orientation of the programme was much more towards undertaking useful work and much less towards training than the Youth Opportunities Programme (though training was seen as a valuable addition to the offerings – the point being made here is that it was not assigned a central role).

There were clear similarities between the Youth Opportunities Programme and the Special Temporary Employment Programme on the one hand and the Job Creation Programme and the Work Experience Programme on the other. The Youth Opportunities Programme was closest to the Work Experience Programme, not only because they both dealt with the 16–18 age group and paid participants an allowance rather than 'the wage for the job' but also because of the similarity between the two programmes in the kind of tasks undertaken and experiences offered. The Special Temporary Employment Programme was closest to the Job Creation Programme, again because of the similarity of the age range covered, the kind of remuneration (a wage rather than an allowance) and the kind of tasks undertaken. In fact, on the introduction of the Special Temporary Employment Programme, the government made it clear that it hoped that Job Creation sponsors would continue with the new programme and suggested that they might like to transfer some projects to it. None of this should be taken to imply that there were no differences between the new and the old programmes. There were a number of differences: there was a clearer delineation of different types of experience and training in the Youth Opportunities Programme and a relaxation of the project criteria in the Special Temporary Employment Programme. Nevertheless, despite these differences, the links between the old and the new programmes were clear and important.

Shortly before the end of 1980 the government announced a number of changes to the then current job creation programmes, changes which came into effect in the following year. Modifications were made to the Youth Opportunities Programme. Some involved the size and scope of the programme: there was to be a 50 per cent increase in the number of places available (440,000 in 1981–82 compared to an increased target of 300,000 in 1980–1), an increase in the budget allocated to the programme from £183 million in 1980–1 to £271 million in 1981–2, and a relaxation of the criteria governing precisely which 16 and 17 year olds were to be offered places on the programme. Other changes related to the training content: following the evaluation of a pilot unified vocational preparation project it was decided to move towards a comprehensive system of vocational preparation for all 16 and 17 year olds. This system was to be designed to provide basic work skills and personal advice and was to be linked to 'off-the-job' training and further education.

More radical changes were announced as far as the Special Temporary Employment Programme was concerned. The Programme was replaced by a new Community Enterprise Programme. The new programme was considerably larger than the old one: it was planned to provide 25,000 jobs (more than double the number of the old programme) and given a budget of £88 million for 1981–2 and £122 million in each of the two subsequent years (compared to an actual expenditure of £45 million on the Special Temporary Employment Programme in 1980–1). The Community Enterprise Programme was also to cover a larger geographical area than its predecessor in that it was not to be restricted to Special Development, Development and designated inner urban areas.

Apart from coverage there were three other main differences between the Community Enterprise Programme and the Special Temporary Employment Programme. The first is that greater emphasis was placed on the need for projects to benefit local communities. Any such work would be considered providing it was work which would not otherwise have been done within two years, and providing the appropriate trade unions supported it. The second is that additional emphasis was placed on training. For example, the project sponsors were to be reimbursed for the cost of the off-the-job training and further education. The third is that increased efforts were made to attract sponsorship of projects from private firms and nationalized industries and funds were to be made available for partnerships in the creation of new enterprises between the public and private sectors.

Many of the other details of the programme were similar to those of the Special Temporary Employment Programme. The programme's target groups were those in the age range 18–24 who had been unemployed for more than 6 months (the inclusion of 18 year olds was a change) and those over 25 years old who had been unemployed for more than one year, and participants were paid a wage based on the 'rate for the job' (subject to a current maximum of £83 a week). Initially the programme was funded for three years.

The changes outlined above had only been in effect for a short while before further modifications began to be considered. At the end of 1981 discussions started on the introduction of a new training initiative for young people. The Youth Training Scheme was introduced in the autumn of 1983 and represented an important change of emphasis in the approach of the government to the problems of the young. The measure has a much clearer training objective than either the Youth Opportunities or Work Experience Programmes, though of course those programmes made provision for training and the Youth Training Scheme intends that some training should be by 'work experience'. The introduction of the scheme was surrounded by controversy: for example, over the level of the allowance to be paid to participants, the early suggestion that young people might be penalized by withdrawal of social security benefits if they did not take part, and the extent to which training would be geared more towards the needs of employers than the young people themselves.

The Youth Training Scheme, though, is to be restricted to the youngest age ranges and young people over the age of 18 will not be eligible. As far as they are concerned, the emphasis on job creation will remain. A new job creation measure, the Community Programme, was announced by the Chancellor of the Exchequer in his budget speech in March 1982 to cover such people. In practice, the

Community Programme has much in common with its similarly named predecessor, the Community Enterprise Programme. One important difference, however, is that the Community Programme offers a lower level of remuneration to participants, and this in itself has been the cause of considerable debate.

9.3 THE ATTRACTIONS OF JOB CREATION

For many years Western governments have relied on what are frequently referred to as 'demand management' solutions to rising unemployment: essentially, the response has been in the Keynesian mould. However, in the 1970s most Western governments were not only facing problems resulting from rising levels of unemployment but were also facing problems resulting from increasing inflation. In many cases reducing the level of inflation was seen as the primary aim of government policy: reducing the level of unemployment was a secondary, though still important aim. This meant that such governments were less keen to deal with rising unemployment by increasing overall demand in the economy, than they had been previously. In practice, many governments took measures that reduced rather than increased overall demand, such as increasing the level of taxation and reducing the level of public expenditure. They looked, therefore, for other non-demand management measures to at least keep the level of unemployment from rising as much as it would have done otherwise.

There are, of course, a number of non-demand management measures available to governments which could be, and in practice, have been used. Some of these were referred to earlier as 'special employment measures'. Among such measures, job creation clearly has had some atttractions.

One of the reasons why it has been attractive is that it seemed to meet the basic policy requirements: that it offered a way of creating employment with less danger of inflationary consequences than would be the case with traditional demand management measures. This is not to say that job creation necessarily does not have any inflationary consequences. Some commentators have argued that it is likely to have a noticeable impact on inflation, though they accept that it is less than would be the case with attempts to generate employment through a general stimulation of demand via monetary and fiscal measures. The detail of this argument cannot be examined here, but it is worthwhile noting that most governments have accepted that job creation schemes will be less inflationary than many other measures because of their relatively low cost.

In practice, the gross costs of job-creation schemes vary enormously between programmes: in the case of the major British programmes the fact that some pay a wage, based on 'the rate for the job', whereas others pay an allowance (normally much lower) has been important. However, gross costs are not the only important factor. Governments have also been interested, and probably more interested, in net costs. An assessment of net costs must take account of savings in unemployment benefits and other welfare expenditures, of increased social insurance contributions, and of increased tax revenue (both direct and indirect). Such estimates have suggested that in Britain net costs have only been about 60 per cent of gross costs for the Youth Opportunities Programme and about 40 per cent of gross costs for the Special Temporary Employment Programme. However, it is arguable that a complete assessment of the costs of job-creation schemes has to go beyond a simple examination of gross and net costs as indicated above and must include some assessment of the secondary and indirect effects of job-creation programmes.

An attempt to quantify such factors has been made for the West German job creation programmes by Spitznagel using an input–output study. This suggested that job-creation schemes may have produced savings equal to or in excess of their costs. It is not possible to conclude that the same would be true in other countries for the savings relate to the particular circumstances obtaining in the country concerned, at a particular time (one factor is the level of social insurance benefits, which are relatively high in West Germany). Nevertheless, Spitznagel's work alerts us to the kind of calculations that need to be made and shows why job-creation schemes have appeared financially attractive to governments.

Another reason for the attraction of job-creation programmes is that they have been seen as a way of dealing with an immediate problem swiftly. Some of the other policies that might be used to alleviate high unemployment take some time before they become effective. Job-creation schemes have been introduced quickly and have been able to offer employment, sometimes within a matter of months. It has also been possible to target job-creation schemes on particular groups and areas much more than would have been possible with a number of the other ways of alleviating high unemployment. In the case of the British job-creation schemes, they have been targetted both in terms of the age of participants and geographical area.

Undoubtedly, it is also important to recognise a political argument. Many governments have believed that it would be unacceptable for them apparently to be doing nothing about rising unemployment. Expressions of concern or a belief that high unemployment was inevitable, at least in the short term, may not have been seen as sufficient from a political point of view. Job creation schemes can be viewed, then, as one way that governments could show that they were 'doing something' and that they were genuinely concerned. It is interesting in this context to note that the first major job creation schemes were introduced in Britain in the mid 1970s when the then Labour government was involved in trying to persuade the trade-union movement to co-operate with a series of economic measures through the Social Contract. At that time many unions were showing increasing concern about the level of unemployment and the reductions of public expenditure and were pressing for action to be taken to deal with employment problems.

However, the attractions of job-creation measures have to be balanced, not simply against the claims of alternatives, but also against a number of less favourable aspects and implications of their operation.

9.4 CONCERN ABOUT THE OPERATION OF JOB-CREATION SCHEMES

Job-creation schemes were developed in Britain, and in other countries, at a time when many governments proclaimed the belief that high levels of unemployment were a short term phenomenon. In such a context job-creation schemes, it was argued, could play a valuable role. Essentially their role was to provide temporary employment opportunities to cover an abnormal situation. When something close to full employment returned the people who had been employed on job-creation schemes would return to the normal employment market and gain permanent jobs. Further, their return to the normal market would be aided by their job-creation experience, for without it they would have suffered a period of unemployment, and research has shown that unemployment can have an adverse affect on a person's desire and ability to obtain work. In some cases it was also believed that job-creation projects might provide an element of training and this might further enhance a participant's prospects of obtaining normal full-time work when the economy improved. Most job-creation schemes, and certainly the British schemes, attached stipulations to job-creation projects stating maximum lengths of stay: prolonged engagement on job-creation projects was felt to be undesirable and unnecessary.

It is crucial to understand then, that job creation schemes have only been designed, in the main, to create short-term employment opportunities. There have been some exceptions, when job-creation schemes have been used as a way of 'pump priming' activity which would be self-sustaining in the long run. In general terms, however, job-creation schemes have not normally been used to create long-term employment opportunities.

In the mid-1970s many economists contested the view that high levels of unemployment were a short-term phenomenon. By the early 1980s most governments had come to accept that such scepticism was justified. Forecasts for most Western nations suggest that high levels of unemployment will continue at least for a number of years. In such a situation the original aims of job creation have been difficult to meet. In the early years a reasonably high proportion of job-creation scheme participants obtained normal full-time employment within a reasonable period of time of leaving their scheme. Exact proportions varied: over 50 per cent of those who participated in the Job Creation Programme and over 80 per cent of those who participated in the Work Experience Programme. In recent years the proportions finding permanent employment have fallen dramatically. Surveys of participants in the Youth Opportunities Programme have shown that less than a third have found permanent employment after leaving a scheme. Undoubtedly one of the main reasons for the reduction in the percentage of people finding permanent employment is that the normal employment market has worsened rather than improved.

Such developments are of considerable concern. They do not simply mean that the programmes may be less effective than they were: they may also result in people who participate in job-creation schemes becoming cynical about their experience. Research has suggested that most participants entered job-creation schemes believing that the experience would assist their chances in the normal employment market and their acceptance and evaluation of job-creation programmes has been centred on this belief. There is a clear danger that if expectations in this area are not met then job-creation schemes will come to be viewed cynically by the people who participate in them and by the agencies and wider community whose support is essential for the effective operation of the schemes. In Britain, for example, many unions have expressed the view that some job-creation schemes have simply been a device for getting work completed which would otherwise have been done by hiring through the normal labour market. Some participants believe that they have simply been used as cheap labour.

Concern about such matters has led to changes in the operation of job-creation schemes. The changes to the British job-creation programmes in 1978 were in part a reflecion of such concern, as have been subsequent reviews. In other countries similar developments have been taking place. One important change in Britain has been to seek to increase the degree of training offered on job-creation programmes and currently, as has been noted, it has been suggested that provision for young people should actually be based on training. In part this change has been a reaction to criticism of job-creation experience. It has been suggested that the extent and level of training has been poor on many previous projects and has not even met the limited aspirations of the project specifications. In part it has also been a reaction to the belief that in a worsening employment market work experience alone is not sufficient to improve job prospects: training is necessary to ensure that participants have specific skills to offer potential employers. Of course, it needs to be stressed that training itself does not create jobs and unless some jobs are being left vacant because of a shortage of skilled personnel, effective training may merely mean a circulation of available jobs rather than the creation of additional permanent opportunities. Further, there must be some scepticism, on the basis of experience with previous training endeavours, whether training programmes are likely to be successful in identifying and meeting employment needs.

As well as changes in job-creation schemes relating to training there have been a number of others designed to enable them to have a longer term impact. In Britain, there has been some relaxation of eligibility rules to enable support to be given to pump-priming activity which could result in longer term permanent employment. The restructuring of the programmes and the allocation of funding has also taken account of the changed employment conditions and has been based on a longer term perspective. Outside Britain, more radical moves have been made. In both Belgium and France the development of a 'third' permanent or semi-permanent labour sector has been attempted, based on novel organizational forms and tasks not currently undertaken by either the public or private sectors.

9.5 CONCLUSIONS

Job creation schemes as currently devised can never 'solve' the unemployment problem and they have not been designed to do so. Nevertheless, they clearly have some attractions and within limits can play a useful role. However, if they are to play such a role then it is important to recognize that changes need to be made. The general economic and more specifically the unemployment situation has changed for the worse since the early 1970s. Few now believe that high levels of unemployment are simply a temporary phenomenon. Job creation schemes need to be changed to meet these new circumstances. Further moves need to be made so that job-creation schemes do not simply provide temporary employment opportunities but also more permanent ones. Unless such changes are made job-creation schemes will be unable to meet the needs resulting from current economic conditions and forecasts.

REFERENCES

Bakenhol, B. (1981) 'Direct Job Creation in Industrial Countries', *International Labour Review*, vol. 120, No. 4, pp. 425–38.

Commission of the European Communities (1980) *Job Creation Schemes in the European Community*, Study No. 80/40 (Brussels: EEC).

Institute of Economic Affairs (1979) *Job Creation – or Destruction?* (London: IEA).

Jackson, M. P., Hanby, V. J. B. (1982) *British Job Creation Programmes* (Aldershot: Gower).

Manpower Services Commission (1980) *Review of the Second Year of the Special Programmes* (London: MSC).

Metcalf, D. (1982) 'Special Employment Measures: An Analysis of Wage Subsidies, Youth Schemes & Worksharing', *Midland Bank Review*, Autumn/Winter, pp. 9–21.

QUESTIONS FOR DISCUSSION

1　Why have British governments of different political complexions introduced and expanded the use of job creation schemes?
2　To what extent have job creation schemes been able to meet the objectives set down for them?
3　What should the links be between job creation and training on the one hand and the education system on the other?
4　How and to what extent do special employment measures differ from more traditional ways of dealing with high unemployment?
5　What is the real level of unemployment in Britain today?
6　How does the British experience of unemployment since the early 1970s compare to that of other Western nations?
7　Why has unemployment been seen as such a cause for concern?
8　Evaluate the claim that recent government initiatives on unemployment (such as the YTS) have been little more than an attempt to 'massage' the unemployment figures.

10 De-industrialization in Britain – an Appraisal

MAURICE KIRBY

In the mid-1970s increasing anxiety began to be expressed in governmental circles at the contraction in employment in manufacturing industry in Britain. In his budget speech in April 1975 the then Chancellor of the Exchequer, Denis Healey, stated his concern at the 'steady loss of jobs in factory capacity year after year' and subsequently his colleague as Secretary for Industry, Tony Benn, observed that in the period 1970–4 there had been a 7 per cent fall in manufacturing employment in Britain resulting in a net contraction of 120,000 jobs in this sector of the economy, a trend which, if it was allowed to continue, would result in the redundancy of nearly 2 million industrial workers between 1970 and 1980 (Benn, 1975). The term that was applied to this process – 'de-industrialization' – became a vogue word in political and economic discussion and it rose to prominence as a result of the work of two Oxford University economists, Robert Bacon and Walter Eltis. In a series of powerfully argued articles in the *Sunday Times* newspaper in November 1975 they drew attention to the considerable change in the pattern of employment which had occurred in the British economy since the early 1960s. (The articles were subsequently expanded and, with a supporting theoretical framework, were published in Bacon and Eltis, 1978a.)

In the period 1961–75 non-industrial employment in relation to industrial employment grew by more than 40 per cent with the public services being the principal beneficiaries. Thus, the number of local authority employees rose by 70 per cent and those in central government by 27 per cent. In marked contrast employment in private services, such as banking and retail distribution, grew by only 11 per cent. Whilst similar trends were observable in other Western developed economies, the rise in service-sector employment was nowhere near as great as in Britain within such a short period of fourteen years. For Bacon and Eltis, as well as Mr Healey and Mr Benn, the loss of industrial employment was a prime cause of 'the disastrous course' the British economy had followed in the period

1961–75. In short, de-industrialization had produced serious structural imbalance in the British economy.

In academic circles the response to the whole notion of 'de-
industrialization' was more circumspect. There was a feeling among
some economists that the concept had 'gatecrashed the literature,
thereby avoiding the entrance fee of a definition, and also avoiding
critical scrutiny at the door' (Blackaby, 1978, p. 1). This view was not
so much the product of the natural conservatism of economists, it was
far more a reflection of the very real conceptual difficulties in applying
the term to an advanced industrial economy such as that of Britain.
Why, for example, should de-industrialization be defined as a
straightforward decline in manufacturing employment when manufacturing output may be an equally valid criterion? Similarly, it could
be argued that manufacturing employment cannot be examined in
isolation and should be related to trends in the total labour market,
reasoning which could also be applied to output, with that of the
manufacturing sector being related to movements in the gross
domestic product. Even if de-industrialization could be defined
satisfactorily in relation to each of these categories, the questions
would remain: is it a cause for concern and if so what action, if any,
should be taken to reverse the process? (Caincross, 1978, pp. 5,6)

10.1 THE BACON AND ELTIS THESIS

In appraising the debate on de-industrialization the starting point
must be the views of Bacon and Eltis. As indicated already they not
only drew attention to the fall in the number of people employed in
industry but also claimed that it was a serious cause for concern and
offered guidelines for economic policies to reverse the trend. Their
fundamental argument is that Britain's relatively poor economic
performance since 1960 and the failure of successive governments to
achieve the triple aims of price stability, full employment and
balance-of-payments equilibrium were the result of the progressive
shrinkage in size of the country's productive base. This was a
development which gathered pace in the 1960s as a consequence of
the growth of the non-market sector of the economy. By 'non-market'
Bacon and Eltis are referring primarily to the service sector, in
particular that part which is controlled by central and local government and which does not produce 'marketable output', possessing a
direct saleable value unlike, say, the banking and insurance houses of
the City of London. The role fulfilled by the market sector in Britain is
vital to the country's well-being. As Bacon and Eltis put it:

Industrial production must supply the entire investment needs of the nation, and a very high fraction of its consumption; for durable goods like cars, television sets and so on, clothing and even quite a high proportion of what workers nowadays spend on food, have to be provided by British or foreign industry. In addition to this, a country like Britain that needs to import a high fraction of its food and raw materials requirements must export more industrial products than it imports. The various private-sector service industries make a valuable contribution to the balance of payments, but this has never been sufficient, and it is never likely to be to finance the food and raw materials that Britain must buy from overseas, so a large export surplus of industrial production is always likely to be needed (Bacon and Eltis, 1978a, p. 16).

It is only the market sector of the economy that is capable of producing real wealth. It is the market sector which underpins the standard of living and, it might be added, sustains the quality of life and the integrity of the realm. Since virtually all the civilized activities enjoyed in Britain, such as art galleries, hospitals and universities, are largely non-marketed, together with the country's defence capability against foreign aggression, anything which erodes the wealth-creating ability of the market sector must be a cause for concern. According to Bacon and Eltis it is precisely this which occurred in Britain from the early 1960s onwards when the 'productive' industrial economy (and this includes the *profitable* nationalized industries) began to be starved of labour and thus obliged to compete for this factor with the burgeoning non-market sector. The effect of this was to set in motion a wage/price spiral to the detriment of Britain's international competitiveness and hence the balance of payments. The mechanism by which this occurred was closely related to cyclical fluctuations in the domestic economy:

It is in the boom when the economy is working most nearly to full capacity that the full effects of previous growth of the non-market sector are felt. High non-market spending can often be afforded in periods of recession when, with spare resources in the economy, extra government spending will not obviously reduce the aggregate real resources available for market sector investment and the balance of payments. However, if extensive and irreversible spending decisions are taken in the slump, supply bottlenecks are reached more quickly in the subsequent boom when private spending also rises rapidly. The balance of payments then deteriorates more massively and earlier than otherwise would have been the case and the boom can be allowed to last an insufficient length of time to get capacity-creating market sector investment... up sufficiently to raise the rate of growth of productive capacity to what is required for a faster growth rate. (Hadjimatheou *et al.*, 1979, p. 405)

For Bacon and Eltis this sequence of events is an excellent description of the course of British economic history and policy for much of the period since 1960. In marked contrast to industrial employment, which did exhibit fluctuations coincident with boom and recession, non-market employment continued to grow over the cycle largely at the instigation of governments which expanded the public sector, especially the health and education services, in order to absorb surplus labour in times of recession but then failed to 'release' these new recruits to central and local government employment when the economy began to recover.

This response to rising unemployment was understandable. Since the publication of the White Paper on employment policy in 1944 there had been an all-party commitment to the maintenance of full employment and with collective memories of the 1930s depression still very much alive, this had come to be the acid test of electoral popularity. In times of rising unemployment it was a comparatively simple matter to recruit redundant industrial workers into the public services, a policy which appealed to the Treasury since this did not necessarily require large capital outlays, certainly far less than the alternative of building extra plant and installing capital equipment on which redundant workers could produce extra marketable output. In fact, there was a 'ratchet effect' at work in the British economy which guaranteed the continued growth of non-market employment at the expense of the market, mainly industrial, sector. Even more serious, however, was the mounting burden of taxation that the growth of the public sector began to impose both on British industry and those employed within it.

In the first instance the pressure on corporate profits reduced the resources available for industrial investment. In the mid-1960s net industrial investment as a fraction of final sales of industrial production was running at a level of 8–9 per cent per annum: by 1972 it had fallen to 3 per cent and had only recovered to 6.8 per cent by 1975 – largely due to the stimulus of North Sea oil exploitation. The effect of this fall in industrial investment was to reduce the rate of industrial growth, which meant that when governments sought to reflate the economy in order to achieve full employment large balance of payments deficits were incurred due to the lack of domestic industrial capacity.

Secondly, increases in personal taxation encouraged industrial workers, and latterly those employed within the non-market sector itself, to demand unprecedented wage and salary increases in order to maintain living standards. This also squeezed industrial profits and had serious consequences for labour relations in Britain, especially under the regime of increasingly stringent prices and incomes policies inaugurated after the sterling crises of the mid-1960s. Finally, the need to retain a higher proportion of industrial output at home due to the resistance of industrial workers to a reduction in their share of marketed output reduced net exports of manufactures and placed additional pressure on the balance of payments. As Bacon and Eltis conclude:

The great increase in non-industrial employment... took resources away from the balance of payments and industrial investment, and this is precisely what Britain could not afford to cut if the country was ever to escape from the trap of an industrial sector too small to provide all that was required of it. (Bacon and Eltis, 1978a, p.18)

For embattled politicians searching for a working diagnosis of Britain's economic predicament the Bacon and Eltis thesis has had much to offer. With its exclusive concentration on the growth of the public sector it provides an alluringly simple yet comprehensive explanation of 'the British disease', from balance of payments problems to unsatisfactory labour relations. In his budget speech in April 1975 Denis Healey called for a reversal of 'the process of de-industrialization', whilst the new leader of the opposition Margaret Thatcher stated in September 1975, 'Every man switched away from industry and into government will reduce the productive sector and increase the burden on it at the same time.' At the Labour Party Conference in September 1976 Prime Minister James Callaghan openly attacked the fundamental premise which had guided economic policy-makers for much of the postwar era:

We used to think that you could just spend your way out of a recession and increase employment by cutting taxes and boosting government spending. I can tell you in all candour that that option no longer exists, and in so far as it ever did exist, it worked by injecting inflation into the economy. And each time that happened the average level of unemployment has risen. High inflation, followed by higher unemployment. That is the history of the last twenty years.

This statement is significant not only as an attack on traditional Keynesian-style demand management but also because it was an implicit acceptance of the Bacon and Eltis thesis that the British economy was suffering from a serious structural maladjustment that was not amenable to 'tinkering' by means of the established policy instruments of demand management, prices and incomes policies, the introduction of new forms of taxation and exchange rate manipulation.

Indeed, the 1974–9 Labour government attempted to achieve industrial regeneration and a return to full employment not by internal reflation but by export-led growth reinforced by the introduction of cash limits on public expenditure in 1976, an interventionist industrial strategy and an 'informal' incomes policy, while the incoming Conservative government in 1979 came to office pledged to reduce substantially the public sector borrowing requirement and having set its face against an incomes policy *per se*, to control the rate of growth of the money supply. It hardly needs to be said that all of these policies have encountered severe difficulties but it is clear that in terms of its impact on Britain's political leaders the views of Bacon and Eltis found favour with a fairly broad spectrum of opinion. In this light it is all the more important to bear in mind that their thesis contains a number of errors of fact and interpretation.

10.2 OBJECTIONS TO THE THESIS

The most obvious problem in applying the Bacon and Eltis thesis to Britain's economic experience concerns the issue of labour utilization. In the first instance it seems inappropriate to speak of the market sector being starved of labour before the mid-1970s at a time when large areas of British industry were noted for overmanning and where the trend rate of unemployment over successive cycles rose inexorably from 1 per cent in the cyclical peak year of 1955 to 2.6 per cent in 1973. It should also be noted that the expansion of public sector employment since the early 1960s resulted in extra employment for females in the labour force, whereas the bulk of the registered unemployed were males. It is an open question, therefore, as to whether the labour absorbed by the non-market sector would have been employed in manufacturing industry (Moore and Rhodes, 1976; see also Thatcher, 1978).

On the subject of the availability of finance for expansion it is similarly difficult to argue that industry was 'crowded out' by the demands of the public sector. Although the pre-tax profitability of British industry declined steadily after the early 1960s there is little evidence to suggest that the expansion of private industry was constrained by lack of access to external funding. As the Treasury pointed out in its evidence to the Wilson Committee on the functioning of financial institutions in 1977,

all the signs are that industrial borrowing has been determined by the level of demand... In the year to mid-February 1977 sterling lending to manufacturing industry increased by about £1350 million, or 24 per cent, while sterling lending to the personal sector increased by only about £200 million, or 5 per cent – a fall in real terms... (Treasury, 1977, pp.52–3) and all of this at a time when interest rates reached unprecedentedly high levels. These observations are in accord with the long-standing view, based upon much empirical evidence, that investment decisions are determined by expectations of demand and profitability rather than the cost of borrowing (Savage, 1978).

As for the burden of taxation imposed on industry, the available evidence is hardly consistent with the Bacon and Eltis thesis since it indicates that there was a significant decline in the effective company tax rate after 1950 and that 'the slow growth of demand, shortages of liquidity and a declining real rate of return on capital have presented a much greater threat to investment than increases in corporation tax' (Moore and Rhodes, 1976, p. 40). In fact, the record of *post-tax* profit-shares for the period 1950–73 suggests that 'there was no long run or secular decline in the share of profits' (King, 1975; for further critical examination of the crowding out hypothesis, see Brown and Sheriff, 1978).

Bacon and Eltis are at first sight on much stronger ground on the issue of personal taxation. It is certainly difficult to refute their argument that the expansion of the public sector contributed powerfully to cost-push inflation to the detriment of profits in manufacturing industry, notably in the period since 1969. But even here a note of warning should be sounded. In international terms, and especially in comparison with some of the more buoyant European economies, the British people have not been excessivley penalized at the hands of the state (Stout, 1978, p. 174). Furthermore, there was no upsurge in the country's economic performance following the Conservative government's programme of tax reductions after 1951, a result which is reinforced by experience in the fifteen years before 1914. As one observer has pointed out the highest rate of income tax in this period was less than 7 per cent and even after significant budgetary changes in 1909 the bulk of taxable earned income paid less than 4 per cent. Yet these were years of stagnation in Britain 'with no rise in productivity, no rise in real wages. The reason for this lay in "other circumstances of the time": [this] may serve to indicate how minor a role taxation may play, among other forces, in the shaping of economic performance' (Phelps Brown, 1977, pp. 10–13).

There are two further weaknesses in the Bacon and Eltis thesis. The first concerns the share in manufacturing employment as compared with experience in other countries. The point here is that Britain has not been alone in experiencing de-industrialization: it has also occurred on a significant scale in the Netherlands, Sweden and the USA. Even those countries with rising proportions of total employment in manufacturing, such as Japan, Italy and West Germany, experienced a check to their 'industrialization' in the years after 1970. After this date 'The change in the rate of change of the ratio of manufacturing to total employment appears to have been in the same direction for most advanced industrial countries' (Brown and Sheriff, 1978, p. 238). Since a rise in public expenditure was a feature common to a number of these countries in the period before 1975 it might well be asked what so distinguishes the British experience from that of other economies? If Britain does not stand out as a truly exceptional case according to the Bacon and Eltis definition of de-industrialization the question remains: what does the term mean in the specifically British context?

The answer to this question leads to the final criticism of the Bacon and Eltis thesis: in simple terms it is unhistorical. Britain's economic difficulties are dated from the mid-1960s following the upsurge in public expenditure and non-market sector employment in the first half of the decade. Yet in so far as Britain's economic decline has its origins in the past – to be precise, a century ago in the final quarter of the nineteenth century when British industry began to lose foreign and domestic markets to overseas competitors – one of the dangers of the Bacon and Eltis approach to Britain's contemporary economic *malaise* is that its very plausibility can be used to justify economic policy prescriptions which are inappropriate or, alternatively, of limited effectiveness. This is certainly not to suggest that historical argument alone is the way to understand contemporary problems or that the extreme complexity of the process of economic decline dictates that history is the most appropriate means to understanding, merely that de-industrialization must be defined in such a way as to take account not only of the present, that is, post-1960, weakness of the British economy but also its long-term causes.

10.3 THE 'CAMBRIDGE' DEFINITION

In the debate on de-industrialization the most appropriate definition of the phenomenon has emanated from Dr Ajit Singh of the Faculty of Economics in the University of Cambridge. According to Singh, in view of the historical evolution of Britain's industrial structure (a net importer of food and raw materials paid for largely, but not exclusively, by manufactured exports) 'an efficient manufacturing sector . . . may be defined as one which given the normal levels of other components of the balance of payments, yields sufficient net exports (both currently, but more importantly, potentially) to pay for import requirements at socially acceptable levels of output, employment and the exchange rate' (Singh, 1977, p. 128 and 1978, p. 204). The latter qualifications are important because in their absence almost any manufacturing sector might be able to meet the criteria for efficiency. Hence, Britain can be said to be suffering from de-industrialization to the extent that the economy, in failing to maintain its share in world trade in manufactures and in the light of the growing import penetration of the domestic market, is 'becoming increasingly unable to pay for its current [full employment] import requirements by means of exports of goods and services and property income from abroad' (Singh, 1977, p. 129). Thus, to improve the balance of payments merely by cutting expenditure might result in the loss of real output with unemployment rising to unacceptable levels. If total expenditure has to be reduced, as this view concedes, it should be channelled increasingly towards British domestic production in order to maintain employment levels and to strengthen the balance of payments in the longer term when the distortions created by the windfall of North Sea Oil have begun to disappear.

It will be noted that the Cambridge definition of de-industrialization is mainly concerned with the contribution of manufacturing industry to the balance of payments. Bacon and Eltis, however, have argued that such an emphasis on the visible trade account ignores the fact that Britain is especially strong in the provision of marketed services primarily through the City of London. Although it is highly unlikely that invisible income alone will ever be large enough to finance essential imports it is possible that as foreign real incomes grow, an increasing contribution to the balance of payments will accrue from the invisible trading account (Bacon and Eltis, 1978b). At first sight this argument is reasonable: Britain possesses a long-standing comparative advantage in the provision of international services, but it is noteworthy that as the decline in Britain's share of world manufactured exports accelerated from the mid-1960s so this was matched (apart from a period of stabilization between 1967 and 1971) by a decline in the share of invisibles (Sargent, 1978). In this light Dr Singh is right to be sceptical about the contribution of marketed services to the balance of payments (Singh, 1977, pp. 121–2).

A further reason advanced by Dr Singh for emphasizing the importance of manufacturing industry at the expense of marketed services is that the former has a critical role to play in the process of economic growth. In historical terms the service sector has been noted for its relatively low level and rate of growth of productivity. But in so far as manufacturing industry is subject to 'dynamic economies of scale' it is hardly surprising that such studies as are available tend to confirm the very close correlation between the rate of growth of the gross domestic product and the expansion of the manufacturing sector in advanced industrial countries. Thus, as Singh concludes, 'from the point of view of the future growth potential of the economy, a shrinkage in its manufacturing sector is clearly a cause for legitimate concern' (Singh, 1977, pp. 122–3; also Thirlwall, 1982, pp. 27–9).

Once the Cambridge definition is adopted, de-industrialization as a phenomenon affecting the British economy in particular is placed in its correct historical perspective. It is in fact nothing more than a new name for a process which began a century ago, the progressive inroads of foreign competition in Britain's overseas markets and the growing import penetration of foreign manufactured goods in the domestic market. In other words, 'Britain's economic problem was not that there were too few producers. It was that the producers were not producing enough, not exporting enough and not investing enough. The problem . . . in fact was much the same as it had been for many years' (Stewart, 1977, p. 277). The 'Cambridge' view of de-industrialization, therefore, has the great merit of drawing attention to the historical causes of 'the British disease' and also the secular decline in the competitive power of British industry both at home and abroad because of *supply-side limitations*.

Between 1965 and 1975 industrial productivity grew faster on average in Britain than between 1955 and 1965. Whatever the reasons for this highly desirable development – the removal of restrictive trade practices, the merger movement in British industry after 1960, wider educational opportunities and so on – Bacon and Eltis have argued that the workers displaced by this productivity growth have been rendered unemployed due to insufficient investment in *extra* manufacturing capacity. Because the public sector expanded so rapidly after 1961 industrial growth was retarded and hence '*employment in Britain has suffered from technical progress instead of gaining from it*' (Bacon and Eltis, 1978, p. 30). But since it is difficult to sustain the view that the weakness of the market sector has been caused by the 'crowding out' effect of public-sector expansion leading to falling private investment via lower profits, it is far more accurate to speak of 'a balance of payments constraint' on the industrial growth rate.

The problem here is that the world income elasticity of demand for British exports has been lower than Britain's income elasticity of demand for imports and it is these unfavourable elasticities rather than excessive non-market investment which have retarded the growth of manufacturing industry in Britain (Thirlwall, 1978). Despite the fact that Britain has enjoyed a substantial labour-cost advantage over its major overseas competitors since at least 1970 large sectors of British industry, from television and audio equipment to motorcycles and cars, have been out-competed. In short, British industry has been unable to exploit the gap in comparative labour costs because of the ability of foreign manufacturers to achieve higher levels of productivity and their greater willingness to adopt technological innovations thus offsetting, in large measure, the labour cost advantage. Whatever the reasons for this – a lack of entrepreneurial dynamism in Britain and/or deficiencies in the vocational training of the 'unqualified' shopfloor workforce – it is certainly the case that the handicap of non-price factors, such as delivery dates, quality of design and reliability in performance has also been a major cause of import penetration and Britain's declining share of the world market for manufactures (Ray, 1978). The example *par excellence* of many of these weaknesses, at least in the public mind, is the motor vehicle industry. A report prepared by the Central Policy Review Staff in 1975 on the volume car production sector showed that in comparable plants in Britain, West Germany, France and Italy, output-per-man was lowest in Britain due to a combination of production line stoppages, overmanning of identical machinery and a depressing number of quality and design faults (CPRS, 1975).

10.4 POLICY IMPLICATIONS

Although the debate on de-industrialization was initiated in the mid-1970s the issues raised are very much alive today, not least because of the catastrophic fall in industrial employment since 1979. The consensus among economists is that the Cambridge definition is the most appropriate in the British context. But it is one thing to define de-industrialization and quite another to agree on the causes, let alone suitable remedies that can be translated into realistic policy objectives and measures. Whilst Bacon and Eltis were extremely careful to emphasize their opposition to 'a crude pro-industry policy' of the kind espoused by Mr Benn and the left wing of the Labour Party, and also the difficulties which would confront *any* British government in building up a prosperous market sector, the great attraction of their approach is that it provides a clear-cut, unambiguous diagnosis. But what does 'supply-side limitations' mean? It is vague enough to open up a veritable Pandora's box of causal factors – weaknesses in the quality of entrepreneurship and trade union leadership, restrictive business and labour practices, failings in the educational system, in the distribution of research and development expenditures, and in the scope and execution of economic policy by successive postwar governments – the list is almost endles. If, as a recent American report concluded, the origin of many of the deficiencies in British manufacturing industry 'lies deep in the social system' (Caves and Krause, 1980, p. 19), this may give some indication of the policy difficulties highlighted by the Cambridge definition of de-industrialization.

There is, however, one issue which has united virtually all contributors to the debate – how to raise the level of manufacturing investment in such a way as to enhance the income elasticity of demand for British goods. For Dr Singh and a number of his fellow Cambridge economists the remedy is to be found in import and currency controls, a policy which is extremely attractive to the 'new left' of British politics in their advocacy of the case for Common Market withdrawal, and greater measures of state intervention in industry backed by the judicious use of North Sea Oil revenues. Another view, which disputes the relevance of protection on the ground that it might invite retaliation and worsen the condition of industry by promoting inefficiency, lays great stress on the need for 'a coherent strategy of export-led growth'. This too would entail more assertive state intervention with a vigorous use of tax and investment incentives to promote the expansion of technologically progressive industries (Thirlwall, 1982).

For those to the right of the political spectrum the emphasis is on the need to bolster British industry's international competitiveness by improving the functioning of the market economy and by reducing the number of claims on marketed output. Inspired in part by the Bacon and Eltis analysis these objectives are to be achieved by a 'rolling back of the frontiers of the state' by means of privatization, control of the money supply, tax incentives and curtailment of the monopoly power exercised by the trade union movement.

More recently, a new view has emerged. Although the economic policies of the Social Democratic/Liberal Alliance are in their infancy it is clear that their main thrust is in the direction of a re-commitment to the principles of the post-war mixed economy in the belief that the private and public sectors are mutually dependent and that any ideologically-based distinction between them is arbitrary and artificial. Thus the markedly divergent policies of the present Conservative government and the Labour opposition can only serve to perpetuate the close link between failures in industrial performance and the growing lack of continuity in economic policy objectives between successive Conservative and Labour administrations since 1964. But whatever the future course of British politics one thing is certain: by their very nature the issues raised by the de-industrialization debate will remain at the heart of political and economic controversy in this country for many years to come.

REFERENCES

Bacon, R. and Eltis, W. (1978a) *Britain's Economic Problems: Too Few Producers*, 2nd ed. (London: Macmillan).

Bacon, R. and Eltis, W. (1978b) 'The Non-Market Sector and the Balance of Payments', *National Westminster Bank Quarterly Review*, May, pp. 65–9.

Benn, T. (1975) 'Tony Benn Writes about Industrial Policy', *Trade and Industry*, 4 April, p. 2.

Blackaby, F. (ed.) (1978) *De-industrialization* (London: Heinemann).

Brown, C. J. F. and Sheriff, T. D. (1978) 'De-industrialization: a background paper', in F. Blackaby (ed.) (1978).

Cairncross, Sir A. (1978) 'What is de-industrialization?', in F. Blackaby (ed.) (1978).

Caves, R. E. and Krause, L. B. (eds) (1980) *Britain's Economic Performance* (Washington, D.C.: Brookings Institution).

CPRS (Central Policy Review Staff) (1975) *The Future of the British Car Industry* (London: HMSO).

HM Treasury (1977) *Evidence on the Financing of Trade and Industry to the Committee to Review the Functioning of Financial Institutions*, Vol. 1 (London: HMSO).

Hadjimatheou, G., Skouras, A., Bacon, R. and Eltis, W. (1979) 'Britain's Economic Problem: the Growth of the Non-Market Sector: an Interchange', *Economic Journal*, vol. 89, June, pp. 392–415.

King, M. A. (1975) 'The United Kingdom Profits Crisis: Myth or Reality?', *Economic Journal*, Vol. 85, March, pp. 33–54.

Moore, B. and Rhodes, J. (1976) 'The Relative Decline of the UK Manufacturing Sector', *Economic Policy Review*, No. 2 (Cambridge: Department of Applied Economics).

Phelps Brown, Sir H. (1977) 'What is the British Predicament?', *The Three Banks Review*, December, pp. 3–29.

Ray, G. F. (1978) 'Comment', in F. Blackaby (ed.) (1978).

Sargent, J. R. (1978) 'UK Performance in Services', in F. Blackaby (ed.) (1978).

Savage, D. (1978) 'The Channels of Monetary Influence: a Survey of the Empirical Evidence', *National Institute Economic Review*, February, pp. 73–89.

Singh, A. (1977) 'UK Industry and the World Economy: A Case of De-industrialization?', *Cambridge Journal of Economics*, vol. 1(2), pp. 113–36.

Singh, A. (1978) 'North Sea Oil and the Reconstruction of UK Industry', in F. Blackaby (ed.) (1978).

Stewart, M. (1977) *The Jekyll and Hyde Years: Politics and Economic Policy since 1964* (London: Dent).

Stout, D. K. (1978) 'De-industrialization and Industrial Policy', in F. Blackaby (ed.) (1978).

Thatcher, A. R. (1978) 'Labour Supply and Employment Trends', in F. Blackaby (ed.) (1978).

Thirlwall, A. P. (1978) 'The UK's Economic Problem: A Balance of Payments Constraint?', *National Westminster Bank Quarterly Review,* February, pp. 24–32.

Thirlwall, A. P. (1982) 'De-industrialization in the United Kingdom', *Lloyds Bank Review*, April, pp. 22–37.

QUESTIONS FOR DISCUSSION

1   What is de-industrialization and why is it a cause for concern in the British context?
2   What is the 'crowding-out hypothesis'? Does it provide a valid description of Britain's economic experience since the mid 1960s?
3   To what extent are the interests of the market and non-market (mainly public) sectors of the economy incompatible?
4   Would you advocate some form of protectionism as a means of reversing the process of de-industrialization, and if so why?

11 The Nationalized Industries

PAUL HARE

11.1 INTRODUCTION: SIZE AND SCOPE

In 1980, public corporations (and this is the legal form that covers most of Britain's nationalized industries) in Britain accounted for 11 per cent of GDP, 8 per cent of employment and 17 per cent of fixed investment. With activities on such a scale, it is to be expected, therefore, that the nationalized industries should attract attention from politicians wishing them to play a part in the conduct of macroeconomic policy, as well as from politicians and others concerned about their economic behaviour and performance.

Most of the present nationalized industries were brought into the public sector soon after the Second World War, but there have been further changes since then. Thus steel was initially nationalized by the post-war Labour government, then denationalized by the Conservatives, and finally renationalized by Labour in 1967. The Post Office was initially a government department but in the late 1960s it became a public corporation and in 1980 this was split into two: British Telecom concerned with telephones and telecommunications in general, and the Post Office to handle letters and parcels. The 1970s also saw the formation of British Aerospace, British Shipbuilders and BNOC (British National Oil Corporation), while the start of the present decade has already seen moves in the opposite direction, towards greater privatization of economic activity. Table 11.1 shows when various industries came into the nationalized sector and indicates whether privatization is likely or in progress. This is discussed more fully later on, in section 11.4.

Now it is important to consider why all these industries were nationalized in the first place and the case for them to remain in the state sector. Many reasons have been advanced for this, some of which are purely economic while others are more social or political. The economic arguments include reference to those situations where externalities (situations where one kind of economic activity affects

Table 11.1   The progress of nationalization

Industry's present name (following most recent reorganization)	Nationalized in (yr)	Privatization plans
Bank of England	1946	
British Gas	1949	Showroom and oil assets to be sold
National Coal Board ⎫ CEGB, Area Boards ⎬ SSEB ⎭	1946 1948 Present organisation dates from 1958	
Hydro Board	1943	
Steel	1951; denationalized 1954 renationalized 1967	
Post Office ⎫ British Telecom ⎬	Government department up to 1969; split into 2 corporations in 1980	End BT's monopoly in telephones and communications equipment
British Rail	1948; BR Board became a separate body when the British Transport Commission broke up in 1962	Non-rail assets (e.g. hotels, offices) to be sold
National Bus Company ⎫ National Freight ⎬ Corporation ⎭	1947; present organization formed in 1968	1980 Transport Act encouraged competition. Management and workforce buy-out. (NFC)
British Airways	BEA and BOAC commenced in 1946; merged in 1972	Planned to sell off all or part but recent losses have delayed this.
Rolls Royce	1973	
British Leyland	1975	Some overseas and non-vehicle assets sold
British Aerospace	1977	Public share issue 1981 (BP-type of solution)
British Shipbuilders	1975	
BNOC	1976	Seperate oil exploration and production and royalty receipts

Note: This table covers the main nationalized industries and indicates the kinds of privatization envisaged, but it should be regarded as a summary only. Some industries/details are omitted.

others in a non-market way, for example, by generating pollution, noise, etc.) or public good considerations (situations where supplying a good to one person also makes it available to others at no additional cost: for example, defence, radio and TV signals) are applicable. More relevant to the nationalized industries, however, is the so-called natural monopoly argument whereby industries benefitting from enormous economies of scale need some form of public regulation to prevent undue exploitation of the monopoly positions that would naturally result from market processes. Similarly, it would be wasteful to allow competition if that entailed duplication of networks supplying individual houses, factories and offices. Either or both of these arguments covers the public utilities and several of the other nationalized industries.

A further argument, only partly economic, supports nationalization as a means of securing domestic supply of some essential good or service. This has been used to preserve jobs or, more usually, to promote rationalization (for example, British Leyland, British Shipbuilders), as well as to ensure supply of goods essential for national defence (British Aerospace). Of course, nationalization is not the only available policy in such cases, since it would be possible for the government to exercise some control over private companies without a formal takeover, provided that the companies concerned remained financially viable. On the other hand, where a major private firm has suffered a financial collapse (for example, BL. Rolls-Royce), the government has sometimes been unwilling to allow the normal processes of bankruptcy and liquidation to proceed, preferring a state takeover instead (see Chapter 7).

If the government is concerned that some service should be available on reasonably standardized terms throughout the country, then nationalization is one means of achieving that. In the case of telephones and electricity supply, for instance, connections in remote rural areas are substantially more costly than urban connections, but the government has insisted that the services should be provided subject to what are normally rather low connection charges (a long way below cost in the more remote locations). Thus to some extent, nationalized industries can be used as instruments of regional policy, areas where supply and/or new connections are relatively cheap, effectively cross-subsidizing the more costly areas.

Finally, it can be argued that nationalization is desirable quite simply in order to strengthen the government's control over the economy. In the 1940s this was certainly one of the key factors favouring nationalization of the bulk of the energy, transport and communications sectors of the economy, though it has been much less important in the more recent wave of state takeovers.

One might think that one or other of these points would apply to most branches of industry and that, as a result, much more of British industry ought to have been nationalized by now. But there are a number of countervailing arguments to nationalization, sufficiently powerful to have induced caution on the part of recent Labour governments, and to encourage the present Conservative government to return some state assets to the private sector, as we discuss in section 11.4. Let us now briefly review some of the main arguments against either nationalization in general or at least further nationalization.

Firstly, it is not certain that nationalization is an essential precondition for improved or stronger government control. Secondly, even for private sector industries in difficulties, the government may well not have access to superior information about likely market development than the private firms themselves. Consequently, a government-induced rationalization (via nationalization) might not be any better than what would have happened as a result of normal market forces (for example, steel). Thirdly, experience in running state industries suggests that there are serious problems of providing an effective organizational framework and suitable incentives to stimulate efficient operation. Because of this, the industries frequently attract criticism (by no means always justifiably) for their relatively low efficiency, over-manning, poor marketing and slow rate of technological progress, and so on. Some aspects of this general area of control over, and government policy towards, the nationalized industries are examined in section 11.2. From what has already been said, however, we can see that debates about nationalization are not at all straightforward. Aside from dogmatic or ideologically based predispositions to favour one particular view, there are strong arguments both for and against nationalization: these need to be weighed up carefully when changes in present arrangements are on the agenda.

11.2 CONTROL AND REGULATION

Each nationalized industry was constituted by means of an Act of Parliament, and in many cases (for example, transport undertakings) subsequent Acts have been used to effect reorganizations. These Acts establish the organizational basis and management structure for each industry, also setting out in very broad terms their objectives (usually in terms of producing/supplying some products or services at a reasonable cost, and with an obligation to set prices in order to cover costs over a period of years), and the residual powers of the sponsoring minister to intervene. In practice, the Acts were never specific enough to guide the industries' economic activities, and they were consequently supplemented by an extensive (and varying) array of other policies and approaches to the question of effective control. These have included the following:

> guidelines based on the White Papers (see below)
> ministerial instructions;
> ministerial approval of investment plans, borrowing limits and cash limits;
> wage and/or price regulation (in periods when the nationalized industries have been co-opted to support the government's anti-inflation policy);
> investigation by House of Commons committees concerned with nationalized industries;
> Monopolies Commission investigations, especially of trading and marketing practices (this is a very recent approach, introduced by the present government).

General macroeconomic policy obviously has an impact on the nationalized industries, just as on any other branch of the economy. Fiscal policy only has any effect in so far as it influences the overall level of economic activity (and hence demand for nationalized industry output) and it has not normally been directed specifically towards the nationalized sector; the principal impact of monetary policy falls on the costs of nationalized industry borrowing. Finally, policies that affect the exchange rate also affect some nationalized industry costs.

The White Papers referred to above have formed the main official policy statements on the economic control and operation of state industry. Papers were issued by the Treasury in 1961 and 1967 and most recently in 1978 (see HM Treasury 1961, 1967 and 1978). All three papers discussed the objectives of the industries, and the approach to pricing and investment policy that should be adopted to meet them, as well as the forms of financial target it would be appropriate to employ. However, the balance between these elements has varied a good deal over time. In 1961, the emphasis lay with the financial performance and commercial operation of the industries, but by 1967 attention had turned more towards economic criteria: marginal cost pricing, and investment decision-taking using discounted cash flow (DCF) methods and a test discount rate (TDR).

Using a variety of arguments, economists had long argued that efficient (and also social welfare maximizing) operation of nationalized industries required that selling prices should be set equal to marginal cost (that is, the extra cost of producing an extra unit of output). Whether this should be short-run or long-run marginal cost might be debatable, but the 1967 White Paper favoured the latter. In practice, many of the industries concerned made little progress in implementing this principle: identifying and estimating the marginal costs of particular activities turned out to be much harder than expected. Thus the costs of an individual rail journey, or an additional phone call depend on the state of the system as a whole, and are almost impossible to isolate from the system. Not only that, but some theoretical economists also argued that if there were departures from marginal cost in some sectors of the economy (for example, due to monopoly, or taxes that affected different branches to different extents), then it might not be desirable for prices to equal marginal costs in the nationalized sector: this view became known as the argument about *second best* policies. Even though its significance is now understood to be a good deal less than originally thought, such arguments certainly helped to inhibit moves towards marginal cost pricing.

However, the debate about marginal cost pricing did lead to some major improvements in two aspects of nationalized industry pricing structures, which may be summarized as two-part tariffs and peak-load pricing. A two-part tariff is a pricing structure involving an initial fixed charge (sometimes called a standing charge, or in the case of telephones, a rental) or a relatively high price on the first units of some product that a household purchases (for example, electricity), followed by a uniform (and relatively low) price on further purchases. In this kind of structure, the latter price may not actually equal marginal cost, but it should be a good deal closer to it than prices based on average cost would be. At the same time, the initial charge helps to raise the revenue required to meet the financial targets imposed on the industry concerned. Thus the wider use of two-part tariffs improved the efficiency of the price structure by moving in the direction of marginal cost pricing, while still retaining enough flexibility to take account of financial requirements.

Peak-load pricing is a structure of prices which recognizes that the costs of supply (especially of largely non-storable and non-transferable goods and services such as electricity, telephones and to some extent public transport) are different at different times of the day or year. For instance, in winter when demand is highest, the electricity system has to bring into use a number of older, high-cost power stations, so even without a precise measure of marginal cost it is clear that costs are higher then. Similarly, during the course of a normal day, there are periods when demand for electricity is low, when only the newest and most efficient power stations will need to be switched into the network and other periods of high demand when less efficient capacity has to be used: again (marginal) costs are substantially higher at the peak than in the off-peak period. A peak-load pricing system would therefore charge users more at the peak than at other times, provided that metering (that is, measurement of usage) was not too difficult or expensive. Another example of peak-load pricing is the telephone system: here the marginal costs to the telephone system of putting through an additional call are not much higher at the peak than at other times, but the costs to customers vary considerably because of delayed or wrong connections, busy lines and so on. So in this case the peak prices are higher in order to encourage some users (for example, private households, who are likely to be more flexible than business users) to shift their demand to the off-peak periods. From a social point of view, however, both the principle and the result are just the same as for the electricity example discussed first. Although peak-load prices may not actually equal marginal costs, it was the marginal cost pricing debate that provided their justification and they now form an accepted part of nationalized industry pricing policy.

Let us now turn to investment decisions where, as already noted, the 1967 Paper favoured DCF methods using a TDR specified by the government. Prior to the White Paper, investment decisions were not often based on formal investment criteria, appealing instead to such non-economic arguments as 'essential for the maintenance of the system', or the 'latest available technology', or 'required to sustain a steady flow of orders to supplying industries', etc.: where formal criteria were employed, they tended to be of the payback period type (that is, working out how long the additional net revenue generated by some investment project would take to cover the initial investment outlays), which is biassed against projects where the returns build up over a long period. DCF methods consider the cash flows generated over the whole life of a project – these will be negative in the early years (because of the investment costs, with little or no extra revenue to offset them) and presumably positive thereafter (assuming that additional revenue exceeds the additional costs of operating and maintaining the new capital). Cash flows arising in different years are discounted using the TDR, and then summed to arrive at what is called the net present value of a project. If this present value is positive, then the project should be approved; otherwise it should be rejected. In these calculations, the TDR was intended to reflect the real rate of return expected on comparable, low-risk, private sector projects: initially it was set at 8 per cent but this was subsequently raised to 10 per cent.

How much effect did this more formal approach to investment decision-taking have on the nationalized industries' practice? Firstly, it is very likely that the opening up of discussion about investment criteria and investment efficiency will have stimulated the industries to think about what they were doing and to try to improve their procedures. Secondly, however, just as for pricing, it proved to be very difficult to implement the new investment appraisal methods in some industries, because for a high proportion of projects there was apparently no way of separating off the effects of an individual project from the system as a whole. Thirdly, for very large and long-term projects like power stations, the main factors affecting the returns to a given project are the level of demand 10–30 years in the future, and the prices at which this demand is met. These depend on so many imponderables (including future changes in government policy) that even the most sophisticated investment criterion has to contend with enormous uncertainties. Finally, there is scope for (and has indeed been) much debate about the treatment of inflation, depreciation and replacement, taxes and subsidies and the most suitable discount rate, so that an acceptance of the new approach to investment still left a lot of problems to be resolved. Overall therefore, the new methods only found applications in a few areas, though the ensuing debates about investment appraisal probably had some beneficial spin-off effects on practice in most of the state industries.

The third issue covered in the 1967 White Paper concerned the financial targets which the nationalized industries were to meet. The industries were normally expected at least to cover their costs, and most were expected to achieve some positive rate of return on net assets. It was widely recognized that such targets could be inconsistent with the Paper's recommendations about pricing and investment criteria (notably in those industries subject to increasing returns to scale where marginal cost pricing would entail financial losses) though the Paper itself had nothing to say on the problem and defended financial targets in terms of the need to ensure managerial accountability on the one hand, and to minimise the nationalized industries' contribution to the public sector borrowing requirement (PSBR) on the other.

Both these arguments returned with renewed vigour in 1978 when the most recent White Paper was issued. In an era when inflation seemed a much more pressing problem than it had been in the 1960s, it was understandable that financial controls over the nationalized industries should be emphasized so strongly. Two forms of financial control were envisaged: cash limits (subsequently known as external financing limits, or EFLs), and medium-term financial targets. These were supplemented by a requirement to earn a real rate of return of 5 per cent on the investment programme as a whole (replacing the earlier project-by-project approach) and a reiteration (actually amounting to a weakening of the earlier position) of the 1967 view about prices now suggesting that prices should merely have regard to marginal cost, as well as to other factors such as the level of demand.

The medium term financial targets were intended to cover 3–5 year periods, and by 1980, targets had been agreed for most nationalized industries, the parties to each agreement being the relevant industry board and its sponsoring minister. Most targets aimed for a certain rate of return on net assets over the agreed period, but that for the Post Office sought a specified return on turnover, and for British Steel and British Leyland it was impossible to do much more than aim to break even in the not too distant future. The status of these targets is not as clear as it should be: in particular, there is room for doubt as to whether they are intended to represent merely the industries' aspirations or whether they are plan targets with sanctions against any shortfalls in their fulfilment.

A further problem with the medium term targets concerns their relationship with the EFLs, these being agreed annually for each industry with its sponsoring department and the Treasury. External financing limits form part of the government's programme for controlling public expenditure in general, introduced under the previous Labour government but strengthened considerably under the present government. The approach involves setting annual cash targets for various components of government expenditure, implying that if the rate of inflation turns out to be higher than was expected when the targets were established, real expenditure must be cut back. Conversely, of course, if the rate of inflation falls more rapidly than expected, a given set of cash limits would allow real expenditure to rise. EFLs are the cash limits that apply to the nationalized industries and, as the term suggests, they constrain not the total expenditure by the industries (as would be the case, for instance, with non-revenue-earning departments like education) but their net contribution to the PSBR. Since in operating these limits, no distinction is normally made between current and capital expenditure, some observers have argued that their recent stringency has contributed to a fall in the industries' investment, that being easier to cut back than current costs, in the short run. This could make it more difficult to achieve rapid productivity gains in the future (though we shall have more to say about that in the next section which looks at the performance of the nationalized industries), and more significantly, it could impede the industries' efforts to meet their medium-term financial targets.

To summarize the present position, therefore, we can say that financial controls over the nationalized industries are now the most prominent type of control, with economic guidelines about pricing and investment pushed into the background as compared to their heyday in the late 1960s and 1970s.

11.3 ECONOMIC PERFORMANCE

In evaluating the performance of the nationalized industries there are
a number of indicators that seem worth investigation and several
comparisons that could be useful. For reasons of space, however, the
discussion of these matters in this chapter will have to remain
extremely brief, little more than a short summary of the main points.

The interesting indicators include output, employment, capital
employed and productivity, as well as more economic factors such as
costs, profits, the return on net assets, and the prices charged for
output. The most relevant comparisons would appear to involve either
manufacturing industries in Britain (effectively comparing public
sector industry with the private sector, or with industry as a whole) or
corresponding branches of industry overseas (so that British nationalized industries are compared with their counterparts in other
countries). The second, international type of comparison is not
discussed here.

In the fifteen years to 1975 (when NEDO investigated the
nationalized industries), total output of the nationalized industries
grew on average by 1.1 per cent p.a., well below the rate for all
manufacturing which was 2.7 per cent p.a. over the period. Of course,
some of the state industries, for example, coal, steel and parts of
public transport, were declining steadily over this period (and
continue to do so in some cases), but others, such as British Airways,
telecommunications, electricity and gas were expanding very rapidly
and it is hard to accept that the overall lack of dynamism in the state
sector was inevitable.

Turning to the decade 1968–78, productivity (measured as output
per equivalent worker) actually fell in coal mining, bus transport, the
postal service, steel production and British Leyland, while only gas,
electricity, British Airways and telecommunications were able to do
significantly better than the average for industry as a whole. This
mixed performance may reflect the real potential of the various
industries, but equally well it could indicate that the management and
control systems in operation have failed to exert enough pressure on
the industries to reduce their costs. That possibility is supported by
the fact that nationalized industry prices have, on average, tended to
go up faster than those for industry as a whole, while their profitability
has been consistently below the industry average despite their price
increases. This also implies that the returns to additional investment
have been low or even negative in recent years, though the poor
general situation masks an enormous diversity of outcomes, from
substantial profits in gas and telecommunications to very large losses
in steel and British Leyland.

To some extent, the recent large losses can be attributed to declining demand resulting from the recession, but that cannot be the whole story. For the recession has really just brought out into the open some serious problems that were previously hidden from view or appeared less urgent: for instance, poor marketing, quality control and reliability that have allowed other producers (both domestic and foreign) to penetrate various markets to the detriment of the nationalized industries. In the next section, we consider some ways in which this situation might be improved.

11.4 CURRENT ISSUES

To conclude this chapter, three issues await examination: the general management/control/incentives problem, privatization, and proposals by the TUC and Labour party for further extensions of nationalization.

East European experience with economic planning, especially in less centralized economies such as Hungary (since the 1968 reforms) illustrate the first problem extremely vividly. The key question here concerns how to stimulate efficiency and responsiveness to social objectives in industries which are shielded from the full force of competitive pressure by a combination of legal monopoly and the absence of any significant bankruptcy risk. Thus in Eastern Europe it has not proved to be sufficient for the planners merely to work out what appears to be a satisfactorily balanced plan and issue corresponding instructions to each enterprise to fulfil it: for the plan itself inevitably depends on information supplied by the enterprises themselves, and they naturally tend to be cautious about what they can do, proposing relatively low output targets and high input requirements. Pressure from the planners can compensate for this to some degree, but without precise information about the true underlying production possibilities their capacity for effective (as opposed to inadvertently disruptive) intervention is bound to be limited. Moreover, the fact that markets for many goods and services frequently operate under conditions of shortage restricts even further the avenues along which pressure can be brought to bear on enterprises to produce efficiently: customers can hardly expect prompt, reliable service from enterprises able to sell virtually anything they turn out (see Cave and Hare, 1981).

With the important exception of the last point, Britain's nationalized industries are in a situation not enormously dissimilar to the above picture. Instead of detailed output targets, the industries receive EFLs and try to operate according to medium-term financial targets agreed with their sponsoring ministries. But, of course, these targets depend on information provided by the industries themselves and there is no reason to believe that the industries will deliberately place themselves in a position where they are especially hard to achieve. There is no need to accuse the industries of deliberate deception here – it is simply the case that the operating costs they actually have to meet are unlikely to be at the cost-minimizing levels one might expect in a more competitive environment. Thus a high EFL or low medium-term profitability targets might simply reflect excessively high costs rather than the sheer impossibility of doing any better. Admittedly, there are only a few industries or activities where direct comparisons with a private sector competitor can be made, but in a recent study, Pryke (1982) found that where comparisons were possible, private sector costs were substantially lower.

This question of finding an incentive system to drive the nationalized industries to produce more efficiently remains unresolved to this day. Even the new regime of EFLs has proved a mixed blessing for its undue emphasis on financial performance in the short term: as suggested above this has tended to encourage cuts in investment rather than the intended emphasis on reducing current costs. While some form of external financial discipline is clearly required for the nationalized industries it is not at all straightforward to devise a good system.

The present government has responded to this problem (among others) by trying to stimulate competition (by introducing various measures to weaken or remove the monopoly powers hitherto enjoyed by the nationalized industries) and by its privatization policy. The latter can cover a variety of concrete measures, including sales of some physical assets (for example, non-rail assets of BR), or sales of some or all the share capital (British Aerospace, National Freight Corporation). (Council house sales are in the same spirit but they are beyond the scope of this paper.) Table 11.1 (see p. 152) summarizes proposals and progress to date.

Is the government right to expect improvements in economic performance to follow privatization? In some instances, the answer is very likely to be an affirmative one. For example, some of the hotels owned by BR had been starved of investment for years because of BR's general financial problems: it is possible that this simply reflected a proper commercial assessment of their viabiliy, but it seems more probable that a sale to the private sector would lead to some attempt at their refurbishment and profitable operation. In other cases (for example, selling off the oil interests of British Gas), it is less clear that any improvement in performance can be expected.

The valuation of public sector assets is always both a risky and a controversial matter when privatization is under discussion. Thus shares in the computer company, ICL, sold off at its more profitable period in the 1970s soon fell sharply as the company ran into difficulties once again, whereas the shares in British Aerospace have risen since they were issued, giving rise to complaints of unfair speculative profits. When assets are sold, the public sector loses the income stream they would have generated in exchange for a single cash payment, while the PSBR no longer has to meet the costs of further investment in the area concerned. Not surprisingly, therefore, there is frequently a conflict of interest when parts of state industry are being sold off, between workers and management, government, potential shareholders and to some extent the customers themselves.

Opposing the current strong trend towards privatization there stands the Labour party and the TUC. The former in particular suggested before the recent general election that it would re-nationalize any major industries wholly privatized by the present government, if it was returned to power. Furthermore, it has even considered proposals to extend nationalization by taking over the clearing banks and some additional branches of industry (yet to be specified in detail). In the light of the above discussion, we should consider how far such measures are likely to contribute to improving the British economy. In my view, the propects would not be very hopeful, for a number of reasons.

Firstly, a major argument for nationalization, as noted earlier, is to strengthen the government's control over the economy: but there are many ways in which this could be achieved that fall far short of outright nationalization. Yet there is little evidence that the previous Labour government was very willing to avail itself of such powers to any great extent, which suggests that nationalization proposals could actually be a pretext for inaction and indecision in more important spheres of policy.

Secondly, there is no longer a social consensus in this country that supports extensive nationalization: many would see it as an outdated response to whatever our economic problems are deemd to be. Since compensation would normally be paid to former owners, it hardly has any impact on the distribution of wealth in the country and the evidence about the efficiency of nationalized industries is mixed, to say the least. Consequently, it seems far more important to ensure that the performance of existing state industries is improved, than that the state sector be extended into new areas. As already remarked, even that modest aim does not present an easy task to any government.

REFERENCES

Beesley, M. and Littlechild, S. (1983) 'Privatization: Principles, Problems and Priorities', *Lloyds Bank Review,* July, pp. 1–20.
Cave, M. and Hare, P. (1981) *Alternative Approaches to Economic Planning* (London: Macmillan).
HM Treasury (1961) *Financial and Economic Obligations of the Nationalized Industries,* Cmnd 1337 (London: HMSO).
HM Treasury (1967) *Nationalized Industries: a Review of Economic and Financial Objectives,* Cmnd 3437 (London: HMSO).
HM Treasury (1978) *The Nationalized Industries,* Cmnd 7131 (London: HMSO).
NEDO (National Economic Development Office) (1976) *A Study of the UK Nationalized Industries: Their Role in the Economy and Control in the Future* (London: HMSO).
Pryke, R. (1982) 'The Comparative Performance of Public and Private Enterprise', *Fiscal Studies,* vol. 3 (2), July, pp. 68–81.
Redwood, J. (1980) *Public Enterprise in Crisis* (Oxford: Blackwell).
Redwood, J. and Hatch, J. (1982) *Controlling Public Industries* (Oxford: Blackwell).

QUESTIONS FOR DISCUSSION

1 Should all or part of some existing state industries be privatized?
2 Should more branches of the economy be brought into the state sector?
3 How would you determine nationalized industry prices?
4 How do governments influence the operation of nationalized industries?
5 To what extent should the nationalized industries be required to meet social needs even where this might conflict with their need to earn adequate profits?
6 In what respects (if any) would you expect a nationalized enterprise to behave differently from an otherwise similar private-sector firm?
7 Should nationalized industries be allowed to seek funding from private capital markets to finance their investment? Give reasons for your answer.
8 Short-run financial controls (external financing limits) and medium-term financial targets for nationalized industries can easily come into conflict with each other. Why do such conflicts arise and how should they be resolved?

12 Competition Policy in Britain

RICHARD SHAW

This chapter examines competition policy from the standpoint of the policy designer. In particular it examines two major areas in which design choices must be made. These areas concern the things to be controlled or acted upon: and the criteria and form of assessment.

The chapter falls into four sections. The first examines the objectives and rationale underlying competition policy. Section 12.2 discusses the alternatives open to the policy designers in the two areas referred to above. Section 12.3 examines British competition policy in terms of the choices made by the designers, and the final section provides a brief summary and some conclusions.

12.1 THE OBJECTIVES AND RATIONALE OF COMPETITION POLICY

Competition policy seeks to make competition effective as one means of contributing to the efficient use of resources in the economy. In essence it is hoped that competition will force firms both to produce the goods and services consumers desire efficiently and to sell them at prices which give the suppliers adequate but not excessive profits. It is further hoped that competition will stimulate technical progress.

The competitive process should achieve these ends in two ways. Firstly, competition should force individual firms to minimize unit costs as a necessary condition for earning profits and surviving in the long run. As part of this process there should be sufficient downward pressure on prices that even efficient firms cannot earn excessive profits. Secondly, firms that are efficient producers of the types and qualities of goods and services most desired by consumers should expand at the expense of rivals with higher unit costs and/or less desired types of goods and services. In this way resources will be transferred from the inefficient to the efficient. This may of course involve the failure or bankruptcy of some businesses as well as the growth of others. The price objective of competition policy is to make this process work effectively.

12.2 METHODS OF ACHIEVING COMPETITION POLICY OBJECTIVES

This section examines the main alternative methods available to competition policy designers in the two decision areas in turn.

(i) What is to be controlled: market structure versus market conduct

Underlying the very notion of a competition policy is the view that market structure or market conduct or both influence the economic performance of industries. This is illustrated in Figure 12.1 which also indicates the major elements of market structure and areas of market conduct. The arrows indicate direction of causation. Thus it is argued that elements of market structure such as the number of sellers in a market affect the pricing and advertising policies of those firms and through these affect the economic performance of the industry concerned. For instance, if there are only two sellers in a market they may decide that it is most profitable for them to reach agreement on their selling prices and their respective market shares so that in effect there is little or no competition for customers or downward pressure on prices. The results of such an agreement may be that the firms can earn persistently large (abnormal) profits or alternatively earn more moderate profits while remaining inefficient producers. In either case market performance may be regarded as poor when viewed from the perspective of consumers, purchasers or other users.

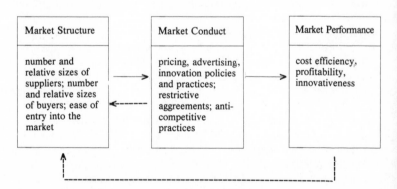

Figure 12.1 Structure, conduct, performance

In seeking to improve market performance in such cases competition policy designers can choose between market structure and market conduct control policies. For example, they can seek to eliminate pricing and market sharing agreements that frustrate the competitive process by (a) banning such agreements, that is by proscribing a particular form of market conduct, or (b) preventing the emergence of market structures likely to lead to such agreements. The two approaches are discussed in turn.

(a) The control of market conduct Advocates of the market conduct approach argue that it is simple and direct, causes little disruption to the firms concerned and is politically feasible. The critics argue that control of market conduct is either irrelevant or ineffective. The price and market sharing agreement example is again used to show the main points of disagreement.

In this example it seems clear that the immediate cause of the poor economic performance is the *agreement* by the two firms not to compete. Hence it may be argued that if such agreements are banned market performance will improve. This is the simple and direct solution referred to above. However, it may also be argued that the problem is the *decision* of the firms not to compete. This decision may be taken by the firms collectively, that is by agreement, or it may be taken by each firm independently. In the latter case each firm decides on its own that it will try neither to undercut the prices charged by its rival nor to win the trade of its rival's traditional customers. These decisions may be based on the belief that any price-cutting or aggressively competitive behaviour will only lead to retaliation and an unprofitable price war. In this interpretation the decision not to compete is the disease and any agreement between firms is merely a symptom. Thus the banning of the price and market-sharing agreement would not improve the market performance because the firms would still avoid price-cutting and aggressive competition. This is the basis for the critics' claim that market conduct controls are likely to be ineffectual.

This claim is supported by two further problems in controlling market conduct:

(i) the difficulty of identifying and policing the prohibited practices, and
(ii) the possibility that substitute, but equally undesirable, practices may emerge to replace any practices that are prohibited.

If particular practices such as pricing and market sharing agreements between firms are declared illegal, this of itself does not necessarily stop firms from engaging in these practices any more than prohibiting drunken driving prevents its practice. Furthermore, even if banning the practice of reaching price agreements does have a deterrent effect, it is possible that firms will merely find some other way of avoiding competition. For instance, they could agree to exchange information on prices in the expectation (but not with any actual agreement) that each firm would avoid undercutting rivals' prices.

The second claim of the critics of market conduct controls is that they are often irrelevant. This claim is discussed in the next subsection on the control of market structure.

(b) The control of market structure Advocates of the market structure approach argue that poor market performance is often caused by the existence of a market structure which makes effective competition unlikely and that the only sure remedy is to change the market structure. The critics of this approach respond by arguing that changing market structure will often be too costly and in any case such government interventions would be politically impractical.

The basic argument for market structure control can be illustrated using the price and market sharing agreement example once again. In this case market structure control advocates would argue that poor market performance is caused by there being too few firms to ensure effective competition. The more firms there are in a market the more likely it is that at least one will think it worthwhile to try to increase its market share. When one firm tries to gain customers at the expense of rivals then other firms will often try to defend their position, and price, and perhaps new product competition will emerge. Because of the likelihood of this occurring the more extreme advocates of market structure control would argue that pricing agreements in markets with large numbers of competitors are bound to break down. Thus if there is a sufficient number of competitors, there is no need to try to control market conduct. This argument is the basis for the contention that if market structure is appropriately controlled market conduct controls are irrelevant.

The same reasoning is applied to other forms of restrictive or uncompetitive practice such as full-line forcing and exclusive supply. In full-line forcing manufacturers insist that retailers purchase quantities of each item in the manufacturer's product range as a condition of being able to buy any of them. Exclusive supply occurs when a seller supplies only one buyer in a certain geographical area, which limits competition between that buyer and his competitors. While both practices have the potential for distorting and restricting competition, the advocates of market structure control would argue that such effects will be minimal if market structure is controlled appropriately. In the case of full-line forcing as long as retailers have plenty of alternative sources of supply they cannot be pressured into accepting full-line forcing. Similarly, exclusive supply by one seller confers no market power when buyers have plenty of alternative sources of supply. Once again it may be argued that control of these practices is irrelevant so long as market structure is controlled.

Three mechanisms for ensuring an adequate number of competitors (sellers and buyers) are usually envisaged. Firstly, the emergence of a concentrated market with only a small number of major firms can be avoided by preventing mergers between firms with significant market shares and between those firms and all others. Secondly, if a concentrated market structure already exists then the competition authorities can break up the dominant firms into two or more independent businesses. Thirdly, however many existing competitors there are, the competition authorities should ensure that entry to the market is easy. This mechanism should provide existing firms with the threat that if they seek excessive profits or are inefficient, new entrants will be tempted into their market with the effect of reducing both the profits and market shares of the established firms. If the threat is insufficient the potential entry will become actual entry and the number of firms in the market will be increased.

The first mechanism of preventing mergers that would lead to markets with either dominant firms or too few competitors, is the simplest to implement. It needs little government interference in industry and would not disrupt the operations of efficient firms. However, its implementation can have disadvantages. Firstly, an important method of rationalizing industry structure to take advantage of economies of scale would be lost. Secondly, mergers and takeovers are one of the means by which resources are transferred from the control of inefficient to efficient firms. While the internal growth (without mergers or takeovers) of efficient firms may also enable economies of scale to be realized and the efficient to triumph over the inefficient, the growth process may be slower and more costly in resource use. Critics of this control mechanism thus argue that mergers and takeovers are desirable features of the competitive process.

The second mechanism of breaking up dominant firms into two or more independent businesses is the most controversial element in a market structure controls policy. Firstly, it would probably be a costly and disruptive process to break up many major firms. Secondly, it would involve a high degree of government interference in industry and this would be unacceptable to many people. For both these reasons critics argue that the policy would be politically infeasible. Thirdly it is not clear how many firms would be necessary to create the conditions in which firms choose to compete vigorously. Indeed the critical number of sellers varies from market to market depending on other factors such as the number of buyers, the rate of market growth and the degree of import competition. If the aim is to increase the number of competitors only marginally then this may not be effective; if the aim is to increase the number substantially then this will be very disruptive and may require the sacrifice of potential economies of scale. Finally, if success in achieving a significant share of a market results in a firm being dismembered it is bound to weaken or even destroy the incentive to compete for market share.

The third mechanism is to prevent the emergence of entry barriers to markets. Unfortunately, this may be difficult or even impossible in some cases. In industries where substantial economies of scale may be achieved when a large fraction of industry output is controlled by a single firm, potential entrants may be deterred by the cost of achieving such a market share. For instance, if it is necessary to control half of the total output of an industry to achieve full economies of scale a potential entrant may predict that its attempt to win such a share would lead to a prolonged price war which it might not win. There is little that competition policy can do about such a barrier except rely on import competition. However, there are other barriers which are the direct result of market behaviour. For instance, an existing major manufacturer may threaten to withhold supplies of all its products . from any retailer who bought any product from a new entrant. Clearly retailers may be deterred from even trying the products of the new entrant and the risk of this happening could deter potential entrants to the industry. It is in this area that the control of conduct and structure meet. It may be possible to identify and seek to eliminate some sorts of conduct which increase entry barriers because this leads to an undesirable form of market structure. It is this feedback effect that is referred to in the broken line causation arrow from market conduct to market structure in Figure 12.1.

Although there is scope for operating a policy aimed at restricting firms' ability to create entry barriers, the same difficulties apply as in the control of market conduct generally. There will be considerable difficulty in identifying and policing any prohibited practices, and firms intent on preserving both their profitability and market shares will often be adept at finding substitute means of making entry to their markets difficult for newcomers.

The conclusions for competition policy designers are disheartening. A market conduct control policy while apparently simple and direct may be ineffective. This outcome is most likely in oligopolistic markets with only two or three sellers. On the other hand, a market structure control policy may be regarded as too costly and politically impossible. The British solution to this dilemma is examined in section 12.3.

(ii) Criteria and form of assessment: absolute rules versus case by case cost-benefit assessments

The second decision for the policy designers concerns evaluation procedures. Once again this is presented as a simple choice between two alternatives although each may be used in different areas of competition policy application.

In the case by case cost-benefit approach each industry is studied separately to examine whether its market structure and/or elements in its market conduct are *on balance* in the public interest. Consider a policy based on control of market structure. The competition authorities may react to the same market structure in two industries in different ways. For instance, they may conclude that in one case a market structure with only two giant, equally sized firms does not provide effective competition and there are inadequate compensating advantages. In another industry with two similar equally sized firms they may conclude that the lack of effective competition is adequately compensated by the benefits in unit cost reduction arising from economies of scale. In the first case the competition authorities might order the breaking up of the two firms in order to increase the number of competitors while in the second the continued existence of the two firms would be permitted.

If the competition authorities were attempting to control market conduct, then the cost-benefit assessment might concern major firms' practice of refusing to supply particular types of retail outlet. In one industry the authorities may conclude that the intention is to prevent the development of price competition by efficient and potential price-cutting retailers (for example, discount stores). In this case the authorities may decide that the refusal to supply is against the public interest and should be discontinued. In another industry they may decide that the refusal to supply some retailers is justified because these retailers do not have adequately trained sales assistants and indiscriminate sales to the public leading to misuse might be dangerous.

The major argument in favour of this case by case cost-benefit approach is its flexibility. As indicated by the examples the competition authorities are able to judge each case on its merits. Its major disadvantage is that such judgements require careful investigation of each case which is inevitably time-consuming and costly.

The alternative absolute rule or *per se* approach requires an initial judgement of the types of market structure and/or conduct that are permissible and those that are not. Any types of structure or conduct that are deemed in general to be against the public interest are then banned. Thus in the case of the markets discussed above with only two equally sized competitors the application of an absolute rule banning

Table 12.1 Control of market structure in British competition policy

Form of market-structure control	Examples	Enforcement agency and control procedure	Form of assessment	Current legislation	Initial control
Increase in the number of independent firms where one controls 25 per cent or more of a relevant market	Splitting up a dominant firm into two or more independent firms	Monopolies and Mergers Commission. Reference by DGFT or government. Government decision following an adverse MMC recommendation	Cost-benefit appraisal	Fair Trading Act 1973	Monopolies and Restrictive Practices (Inquiry and Control) Act, 1948.
Prohibition of mergers where assets to be taken over greater than £15 million or the firm enhances its control of 25 per cent or more of a relevant market	Prevention of merger between two firms each with a 20 per cent share of the UK market for same product	Monopolies and Mergers Commission. Preliminary assessment by DGFT and the Mergers Panel.[1] Reference by government to MMC on recommendation by DGFT. Government decision following an adverse MMC recommendation	Cost-benefit appraisal	Fair Trading Act 1973	Monopolies and Mergers Act, 1965

Table 12.1 Control of market structure in British competition policy (continued)

Amendment to barriers to entry to a market	Reduction in advertising expenditure by established firms; reduction in import duties; cessation of refusal to supply particular classes of retailer	Monopolies and Mergers Commission. Monopolies reference by DGFT or government. Government decision following an adverse MMC recommendation	Cost-benefit appraisal	Fair Trading Act 1973	Monopolies and Restrictive Practices (Inquiry and Control) Act, 1948
Amendment to barriers to entry to a market caused by anti-competitive practices by firms with a turnover of £5 million or more, or a 25 per cent share of a relevant market	Cessation of refusal to supply particular classes of retailer; full-line forcing; predatory pricing; price discrimination	DGFT and Monopolies and Mergers Commission. (i) DGFT investigation and if adverse report may seek undertakings from the firm. (ii) Competition reference by DGFT to MMC if satisfactory undertakings from the firm not obtained. Government decision following an adverse MMC recommendation	Cost-benefit appraisal	Competition Act 1980	Competition Act 1980

Notes: DGFT: Director General of Fair Trading; MMC: Monopolies and Mergers Commission; 1: Mergers Panel – a government interdepartmental committee.

12.2   Control of market conduct in British competition policy

Types of market conduct	Examples	Enforcement agency and control procedure	Form of assessment	Current legislation	Initial control
Agreements between producers and suppliers of goods and services	Prices to be charged, resale prices to be recommended, terms and conditions on which goods and services are supplied or acquired; quantities or description of goods to be produced, supplied or acquired	Restrictive Practices Court. Registration of agreement with DGFT required. DGFT submits the case to the Court. Court decision	Cost-benefit appraisal with the presumption that the agreement is contrary to the public interest	Restrictive Trade Practices Act, 1976	Restrictive Trade Practices Act, 1956 for goods. Fair Trading Act, 1973 for services
Information agreements between producers and suppliers of goods and services	Prices and terms and conditions of supply	Restrictive Practices Court. Registration of agreement with DGFT required. DGFT submits the case to Court. Court decision	Cost-benefit appraisal with the presumption that the agreement is contrary to the public interest	Restrictive Trade Practices Act, 1976	Restrictive Trade Practices Act, 1968 for goods. Fair Trading Act, 1973 for services

12.2 Control of market conduct in British competition policy (continued)

Collective enforcement of resale price maintenance	Agreements between firms to withhold supplies, or to supply on less favourable terms, or to recover penalties as a means of enforcing resale price maintenance	Restrictive Practices Court	Absolute rule per se illegal	Resale Prices Act, 1976	Restrictive Trade Practices Act, 1956
Resale price maintenance by individual firms	Contract for sale or agreement establishing the minimum prices for the resale of goods	Restrictive Practices Court. Practice illegal unless exception granted by the Court	Cost-benefit appraisal with the presumption that the agreement is contrary to the public interest	Resale Prices Act, 1976	Resale Prices Act, 1964
Anti-competitive practices by firms with a turnover of £5 million or more, or a 25 per cent share of a relevant market	Price discrimination or predatory pricing, vertical price squeezing, exclusive supply, selective distribution, full line forcing, tie-in sales	DGFT and Monopolies and Mergers Commission (i) DGFT investigation and if adverse report may seek undertakings from the firm; (ii) Competition reference by DGFT to MMC if satisfactory undertakings from the firm not obtained. Government decision following an adverse MMC recommendation	Cost-benefit appraisal	Competition Act 1980	Competition Act 1980

12.2 Control of market conduct in British competition policy (continued)

Prices where it is of major public concern and affects consumers		DGFT and Secretary of State. Investigation of prices by DGFT on direction by Secretary of State. Report to Secretary of State. Any further action would require anti-competitive practice reference or monopoly reference. See procedures above	Cost-benefit appraisal	Competition Act, 1980	Prices and Incomes Policies 1965–70 1973–9
Efficiency and costs of service provided, possible abuse of monopoly situation by nationalized industries and other public bodies (e.g. Agricultural Marketing Boards, Water Boards)	Costs and efficiency of the Central Electricity Generating Board	Monopolies and Mergers Commission. Reference by government. Government decision following an adverse MMC recommendation	Cost-benefit appraisal	Competition Act, 1980 and Fair Trading Act, 1973	1967–70 under Prices and Incomes Acts, 1966 and 1967

such a structure would lead to the breaking up of those firms in both industries irrespective of the compensating benefits from economies of scale. Similarly, if the practice of refusal to supply is normally felt to be against the public interest it may be banned in all cases notwithstanding possible arguments in its favour in some instances.

The major advantages of the absolute rule approach are its relative simplicity and the saving in costs for both competition authorities and firms in avoiding case by case appraisals. Its adoption may also lead to a rapid elimination of any market conduct practices that are considered to be against the public interest. Its major disadvantage is that in ignoring offsetting benefits the absolute rule approach risks prohibiting the development of market structures and types of conduct which in particular cases would be in the public interest.

12.3 UK COMPETITION POLICY IN PRACTICE

The current situation in Britain is summarized in Tables 12.1 and 12.2 for controls of market structure and market conduct respectively. Each table shows the area controlled, the enforcement agency and control procedure, the form of assessment involved and the relevant legislation. The two decision areas for policy designers discussed in the previous section are examined in turn. However as a preliminary to this discussion the organizational structure of the British competition authorities is outlined.

Four main enforcement agencies are currently active in competition policy in Britain. These are: government departments; the Director General of Fair Trading together with his Office of Fair Trading; the Monopolies and Mergers Commission (MMC); and the Restrictive Practices Court (the Court). The central agency is the Office of Fair Trading (OFT) headed by the Director General of Fair Trading (DGFT). It has a general responsibility for overseeing the operation of competition policy; it maintains the register of agreements between firms and both refers cases to the Court and acts as the prosecution in restrictive practices and resale price maintenance cases before the Court; it may also make references to the MMC and in the case of adverse decisions being accepted by the government it has to implement them; and finally the DGFT has discretionary powers to intervene directly to cause firms to modify or discontinue their use of anti-competitive practices or to modify their agreements so that they become acceptable. An examination of the control procedures shown in Tables 12.1 and 12.2 shows the pivotal position of the OFT and its head, the director general.

The Restrictive Practices Court is a court of law. The Court membership comprises a judge and at least two appointed members. The judge alone makes decisions on matters of law but decisions on the evaluation of cases are taken by majority verdict. As may be seen from Table 12.2 the Court is the major enforcement agency for restrictive practices agreements between firms, and for resale price maintenance. Apart from closely defined situations such as an agreement that has already been terminated or where the government has accepted the advice of the DGFT that an agreement has insignificant effects, all agreements must be referred to the Court. Following an adverse judgement the Court orders the cessation of the offending agreement. Subsequent continued operation of such an agreement would make the parties liable to a fine for contempt of court.

The Monopolies and Mergers Commission is an administrative tribunal. It is the major enforcement agency responsible for control of statutory monopolies (where a firm controls at least 25 per cent of a relevant market), mergers and anti-competitive practices. The power of the MMC is however limited both by its only being able to consider cases referred to it by the government or the DGFT, and in the case of adverse judgements its recommendations only being submitted to the government for the final decision.

Finally, the government retains the power to make references to the MMC, or to veto references made by the DGFT, and to make the final decisions on remedies in MMC cases. These powers enable the government to determine whether competition policy enforcement is pursued vigorously or not. Only in the areas where the Restrictive Practices Court has jurisdiction is government power largely curtailed.

It is apparent from Tables 12.1 and 12.2 that British competition policy in principle seeks to control both market structure and market conduct. However, in practice the control is primarily of market conduct with market structure control being notably lax. In spite of the existence of the necessary powers and the existence of dominant firms in many industries, up to 1981 no firms had been broken up in an attempt to increase the number of competitors.[1] Further, even the power to stop mergers has been very sparingly used. Thus between 1965 and 1978 only forty three intended mergers[2] were referred to the MMC as a first step in the process required for preventing a merger. In the same period approximately 1500 mergers satisfied the legal requirements for such a referral. Only the third market structure control mechanism of attempting to restrict firms' ability to construct barriers to entry has been seriously implemented. However, as indicated earlier, this largely involves stopping firms pursuing particular forms of market conduct. The general failure to enforce market structure controls concerning numbers of competitors reflects primarily a belief that the benefits arising from large firms often outweigh any dangers of monopolistic exploitation arising from concentrated market structures with few sellers. While evidence exists of both economies of scale, including the technological progressiveness of some large firms, and monopolistic exploitation, economic research has not so far shown either to predominate. Secondly, the MMC may have drawn back from recommending the break up of dominant firms because of doubts about government willingness to implement such a radical solution.

However, the need for some action has been generally accepted and this has taken the form of market conduct control. Four major types of conduct have been involved: agreements between suppliers on a wide range of matters (see Table 12.2); resale price maintenance; uncompetitive practices; and prices. Control has been vigorously and consistently applied with respect to agreements between firms since the Restrictive Trade Practices Act, 1956. Similarly, resale price maintenance has been firmly brought under control since the Resale Prices Act, 1964. However, although some attempts to control anti-competitive practices by dominant firms have been made ever since the inception of UK competition policy in 1948, systematic control has only become possible through the Competition Act, 1980. The latter made it possible for the DGFT, and perhaps the MMC, to investigate individual practices such as full-line forcing by a particular firm without at the same time investigating all aspects of the firm's behaviour in a full-scale industry reference. Finally, firms' pricing behaviour has typically only been subject to control under the interventionist Labour governments of the 1960s and 1970s. In the current legislation price controls, while retained, are almost certainly relegated in practice to interventions of last resort where market structure clearly prevents the emergence of effective competition.

One indicator of the effectiveness of the conduct controls is provided by the statistics on registered agreements. By the end of 1981 3940 agreements between firms relating to goods had been registered and of these 3231 had been terminated. Only 658 references to the Restrictive Practices Court and only 39 adverse judgements in the 50 contested cases were needed to achieve this massive abandonment of agreements. In most cases firms recognized from the precedents set in early cases that the Court would probably give an adverse judgement and so abandoned their agreements without incurring the cost of a court case. Many of the registered agreements still remaining have been deemed of little economic significance and the DGFT has been discharged of the responsibility to refer them to the Court. It is still too early to assess the control of agreements relating to services since these were only brought within the scope of the legislation in 1973. Nevertheless the indications are that there will be large numbers of agreements which are abandoned or have their restrictions removed without being contested in the Restrictive Practices Court.[3] The control of resale price maintenance (RPM) – that is the practice of manufacturers specifying minimum prices at which their products may be resold by distributors – appears to be another success story. RPM, which applied to about 20–5 per cent of consumers' expenditure in 1960, has virtually disappeared. Once again only four Restrictive Practices Court cases resulting in two adverse decisions (confectionery and footwear) were needed to achieve the wholesale abandonment of the practice though other factors were also very important. Among these was the development of chains of retailers that were too powerful to succumb to insistence on RPM by manufacturers.

However, these apparently impressive achievements by the Restrictive Practices Court may be misleading. The purpose of conduct controls is to ensure that competition is effective. The mere abandonment of agreements or the dropping of RPM does not ensure this. Some of the registered agreements may have been replaced by unregistered and secret agreements or tacit collusion between firms. Similarly RPM has been replaced by the practice of recommending prices which in turn become the effective minimum resale price. Indeed one interpretation of the ever widening scope of conduct controls reflected in the stream of legislation passed since 1956 is that another form of anti-competitive practice springs up as soon as one is controlled. The Competition Act, 1980, is in part a recognition of this problem. Instead of specifying particular *forms* of conduct to be controlled, such as refusal to supply or full line forcing, the Act defines a practice as anti-competitive if it has the 'effect of restricting distorting or preventing competition' in a particular situation. However, even this move to an '*effects*' approach[4] does not remove the problems of identifying anti-competitive conduct or of forcing firms to compete if they do not want to.

The achievements of the Monopolies and Mergers Commission in controlling market conduct do not even have the virtue of impressive statistics. Between 1959 (when the MMC effectively ceased to be concerned with agreements between firms following the Restrictive Practices Act, 1956) and 1978 the MMC produced only 32 reports concerned with monopolies and oligopolies in the supply of goods.[5] Unlike the Restrictive Practices Court cases, however, the 29 adverse judgements of at least some aspects of firms' behaviour had no implications for market conduct beyond the industries actually investigated. Furthermore, even for the small number of industries concerned it remains uncertain whether the resulting *apparent* changes in behaviour have made competition more effective. As with all attempts to control market conduct it is possible that the firms have substituted other forms of anti-competitive practice and are still choosing not to compete with each other.

In the second decision area the policy designers have opted predominantly for the case by case cost-benefit investigation approach (see Tables 12.1 and 12.2). Only the collective enforcement of RPM has been absolutely prohibited. In all other cases there is provision for a case by case assessment though for two types of conduct this is effectively restricted. Firstly, RPM operated by individual firms is also prohibited unless the firms concerned obtain exemption from the Restrictive Practices Court. Since this exemption is likely to be difficult to obtain RPM is close to being absolutely prohibited. Secondly, most agreements between firms, including information agreements on prices, are assessed under the basic presumption that they are against the public interest. The onus is on the firms to satisfy the Restrictive Practices Court that benefits obtained under specified defences outweigh the disadvantages. Following some early adverse decisions by the Court not many firms have availed themselves of the opportunity for individual case assessment. This is perhaps not surprising when the costs of defending a restrictive agreement before the Court have been reported to run from 'tens of thousands of pounds' up to £0.25 million in the larger and more complicated cases. For the economy as a whole the resource costs will be approximately doubled since the DGFT, and thus the taxpayer, will spend similar amounts in taking the case to court. Concern about costs and the ponderous nature of competition controls have also extended to the MMC where reports on monopoly references take up to eighteen months or even two years to complete. In view of this the provision under the Competition Act of 1980 for less costly and more speedy discretionary action by the DGFT in anti-competitive practices cases is certainly to be welcomed.

12.4 SUMMARY AND CONCLUSIONS

British competition policy operates primarily by control of market conduct with only the most tentative attempts to control market structure. While the emphasis on conduct is generally acceptable politically and has had some success in increasing competition it also carries the risk that in some cases competition policy will be ineffective. This is most likely in markets dominated by only two or three major competitors. It would at the very least be sensible to use the existing merger controls more actively to prevent the further development of concentrated market structures with few or dominant sellers.

The policy is implemented almost entirely by case by case cost-benefit appraisals of market conduct. While this approach reduces the risk of wrongly preventing beneficial practices, it has led to a costly and cumbersome controls procedure. The recently increased scope for discretionary action by the DGFT over anti-competitive practices is a useful step both in increasing the flexibility of the controls procedure and in reducing its costs.

NOTES

1   Two recent cases may indicate a limited change in policy. Firstly the MMC in its 1980 report on the supply of gas appliances included among its recommendations an option that the British Gas Corporation 'should discontinue its retailing functions and that the retailing of gas appliances should become exclusively a private-sector activity'. This option was accepted by the government but it has still to be implemented. Secondly, the MMC recommended in its report on 'Roadside Advertising Services', 1981, that British Posters Ltd. a selling agency for its ten member companies, should be abandoned. This recommendation was implemented early in 1982.
2   Excluding newspaper mergers where different legislative provisions apply.
3   Although services were brought within the scope of the legislation in 1973 agreements only had to be registered from 1976. By the end of 1981, 686 agreements relating to services had been registered of which 129 had already been terminated. This change occurred with only five references to the Court. There has still to be a judgement on the first case.
4   The 'effects' approach is used in EEC Competition Policy under the Treaty of Rome. EEC policy is directly applicable to the UK. See Shaw (1982).
5   The MMC also produced investigatory reports on 'Parallel Pricing', 'Refusal to Supply', 'Professional Services', and 'Recommended Resale Prices'.

REFERENCES

Department of Prices and Consumer Protection (1979) *A Review of Restrictive Trade Practices Policy, A Consultative Document*, Cmnd 7512 (London: HMSO).
Department of Prices and Consumer Protection (1980) *A Review of Monopolies and Mergers Policy, A Consultative Document*, Cmnd 7198 (London: HMSO).

Department of Trade (1981) *Annual Report of the Director General of Fair Trading, January–December 1980*, HC 354 (London: HMSO).

Department of Trade (1982) *Annual Report of the Director General of Fair Trading, January–December 1981*, HC 434 (London: HMSO).

Prest, A. R. and Coppock, D.J. (eds.) (1982) *The UK Economy: A Manual of Applied Economics*, 9th ed. (London: Weidenfeld & Nicolson).

Shaw, S.A. (1982) 'EEC Competition Policy and the European Synthetic Fibres Industry', Stirling University, mimeo.

QUESTIONS FOR DISCUSSION

1   What types of market conduct affect market structure?
2   How does market performance affect market structure?
3   How should the effectiveness of competition policy instruments be measured?
4   If it is sensible to denationalize or privatize public sector monopolies, is it not also sensible to restore competition by breaking up both private and public sector monopolies?
5   What are the main difficulties in attempting to improve market performance through the control of restrictive practices?
6   Critically examine the view that the failure by the UK competition authorities to control market structure has inevitably led to the ineffectiveness of competition policy.
7   Describe any *two* forms of restrictive practice. Examine how these restrictive practices may be expected to distort competition and impair market performance.

Index